EXPOSITORY STUDIES IN JOB

Titles by Ray C. Stedman in the "Discovery Books" Series:

Authentic Christianity (2 Corinthians 2:14–6:13)
Behind History (Parables of Matthew 13)
Death of a Nation (Book of Jeremiah)
Jesus Teaches on Prayer
The Queen and I (Book of Esther)
Riches in Christ (Ephesians 1–3)
The Servant Who Rules (Mark 1–8)
The Ruler Who Serves (Mark 9–16)
Spiritual Warfare (Ephesians 6:10–18)
Understanding Man (Genesis 2–3)
From Guilt to Glory (Romans) Vols. 1 and 2
Expository Studies in 1 John

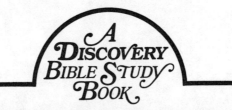

A DISCOVERY BIBLE STUDY BOOK

EXPOSITORY STUDIES IN JOB

BEHIND SUFFERING

RAY C. STEDMAN

WORD BOOKS
PUBLISHER
4800 WEST WACO DRIVE
WACO, TEXAS
76703

Discovery Books are published by Word Books, Publisher, in cooperation with Discovery Foundation, Palo Alto, California.

ISBN 0-8499-2932-6
Library of Congress Catalog Card Number: 80-54546

Printed in the United States of America

Contents

1. The Test (Job 1)   9
2. The Pressure of Pain (Job 2)   25
3. Is It Better to Die? (Job 3–7)   38
4. The Folly of Platitudes (Job 8–14)   55
5. Help from on High (Job 13–19)   72
6. Why Doesn't God Intervene? (Job 20–26)   88
7. The Wrong of Self-defense (Job 27–31)   107
8. Youth Answers Age (Job 32, 33)   123
9. Your God Is Too Small (Job 34–37)   137
10. The God of Nature (Job 38, 39)   155
11. The Nature of God (Job 40,41)   173
12. The New Beginning (Job 42)   188
13. Lessons from Job   203

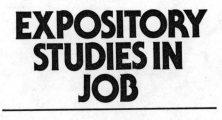

EXPOSITORY STUDIES IN JOB

1

The Test

The Book of Job is perhaps the oldest book in the Bible. No one knows who wrote it. Some scholars think it may have been written by Moses—and perhaps it could have been—while some date it as late as the time of Solomon. But one thing is certain, it was given to us by the Holy Spirit. A very profound book, in many ways it touches upon certain themes more deeply than any other book of the Bible. It is also very beautiful, written in majestic, glorious language.

Job was a real man, not a mythological figure. He is mentioned by Ezekiel and is classified as one of the three great men of the Old Testament, along with Noah and Daniel. He is mentioned also in the New Testament by James, who refers to Job's patience and steadfast endurance. According to the opening verse, Job lived in the land of Uz and was probably one of the most prominent citizens of that land. He may well have been a contemporary of

Abraham, and if so, this book goes back to the very beginnings of biblical history

As we will see, Job is a kind of epic poem, very much like Homer's *Iliad* and the *Odyssey*. It may have been presented at times as a drama in which actors recited the parts of the different characters in the book. Most of the book is poetry but it begins and ends with prose sections which are like program notes given to an audience.

Blameless, But Not Sinless

Chapter 1 gives us the setting, and introduces Job, the main character. We are told first of his piety (v. 1):

> There was a man in the land of Uz, whose name was Job; and that man was blameless and upright, one who feared God, and turned away from evil.

The most noteworthy thing about Job was his godliness; he feared God. The Revised Standard Version also says he was blameless, and many who have read that have taken it to mean that Job was sinless. But one can be sinful and still be blameless if he has learned how to handle his sin the way God tells him to. Evidently Job had learned how to handle sin, so in that sense he was blameless.

I do not think, however, that this is the best translation of the Hebrew word that appears here. The word means "a complete, or well-balanced man." Job was well-balanced because he feared God. He was not a materialist; he did not look on life as merely a means of getting ahead in the world. Job was also aware of God; he saw God's hand in everything he did. That made him a complete man.

This is not to say that Job was a theologian, however. He was a practical, down-to-earth man. I think these terms are best explained by the last part of verse 1: "[He] feared God, and turned away from evil." That is, he was complete because he feared God; he was upright because he turned away from evil.

The second thing we are told is that Job was very prosperous (v. 3):

> He had seven thousand sheep, three thousand camels, five hundred yoke of oxen, and five hundred she-asses, and very many servants; so that this man was the greatest of all the people of the east.

Job was well known for his prosperity. He sounds like a rich Texas cattleman! God gives riches at times, and riches are not necessarily evil although we are warned about the danger and deceitfulness of them. Here was a man whom God had made rich.

The last personal thing we are told about Job is his love, his fatherly concern for his children (v. 4):

> His sons used to go and hold a feast in the house of each on his day [on his birthday] and they would send and invite their three sisters to eat and drink with them. And when the days of the feast had run their course, Job would send and sanctify them, and he would rise early in the morning and offer burnt offerings according to the number of them all; for Job said, "It may be that my sons have sinned, and cursed God in their hearts." This Job did continually.

That little phrase, "cursed God in their hearts," becomes a kind of theme to the Book of Job. Ultimately, that is the test to which Job himself is put: Will he curse God in his heart? This was a matter of great concern to Job about his children. He had seven sons, and as each had a birthday, that meant seven times a year they had a feast to which they invited their sisters. What Job did, according to the record, was the equivalent of our holding a special time of prayer for someone about whom we have a concern. Job offered burnt offerings, because he recognized that his children needed spiritual help most when things were going well, not during times of stress. This indicates a great deal of spiritual insight on the part of Job. He knew that the pressure to deny God, to forsake God, comes most strongly when things are going well.

Job did not offer a sin offering, because that was something only the sinner himself could do. (Sin offerings are of no value if one does not personally repent of the sin.) But Job offered a burnt offering which, in the Scriptures, is always a symbol of total dedication to God, a recognition of God's rightful ownership of men. When Job made this offering he was expressing the burden of his heart for his children, that they might be wholly God's. He was praying for them by means of this burnt offering. So we have a picture of Job as a godly man, a great landowner, and a good father.

The Curtain Is Lifted

In verse 6 the scene suddenly shifts to that world of invisible realities which, in the New Testament—especially in the Epistle to the Ephesians—is called "the heavenlies." This sphere is not off in space somewhere; it is right around us but we are separated from it by an invisible barrier so that we cannot see what is going on in that world, where God and Satan, angels and demons, function. Suddenly the curtain is lifted. Just as the eyes of the servant of Elisha were opened at the prophet's prayer so that he saw the mountain ringed about with the chariots of God, so now our eyes are suddenly opened to this drama. We see what is going on behind the scenes, what Job himself could not see (vv. 6–12):

> Now there was a day when the sons of God came to present themselves before the Lord, and Satan also came among them. The Lord said to Satan, "Whence have you come?" Satan answered the Lord, "From going to and fro on the earth, and from walking up and down on it." And the Lord said to Satan, "Have you considered my servant Job, that there is none like him on the earth, a blameless and upright man, who fears God and turns away from evil?" Then Satan answered the Lord, "Does Job fear God for nought? Hast thou not put a hedge about him and his house and all that he has, on every side? Thou hast blessed the work of his hands, and his possessions have increased in the land. But put forth thy hand now, and touch all that he has, and he will curse thee to thy face." And the Lord said to Satan, "Behold, all that he has is in your power; only upon himself do not put forth your hand." So Satan went forth from the presence of the Lord.

This is surely a most impressive scene, similar to what John describes in the fourth chapter of the Book of Revelation, where he sees tens of thousands and thousands upon thousands of angels gathered in the great audience chamber of heaven, in the very presence of God himself. The angels here are called the sons of God because, like Adam, they were a direct creation of God's hand. But, unlike Adam, they were not given the capacity nor the command to multiply and produce others like themselves. No one knows how many angels there are. There seem to be countless numbers of them, but all of them were created directly by God, and in this instance, were present before God to give a report of their activities.

Surely we need to fling back the borders of our imagination in viewing a scene like this, and realize that God is interested in far more than this little dark planet of ours. As scientists look at the universe today there are many guesses as to how many other planetary systems there are like ours; how many other inhabitable worlds are out there among the millions of galaxies that span the heavens. No matter how many there are, one thing is clear, both from science and Scripture: it all adds up to one universe, one place, and God is in control of it all.

These ministering angels came to report, and in the midst of them is Satan. *Satan* means "the Adversary," and that is how he first appears in the Book of Job. Although he is there with all the angels, he has obviously already fallen. In the Books of Isaiah and Ezekiel we are told how he fell. Once the greatest of the angels, Lucifer, lifted up by pride, has become the enemy of God, the rebel within the kingdom of God. You can see him sauntering about among the angels, hands in his pockets, picking his teeth, disdainful of all the rest, looking for an opportunity to accuse.

Access to God

The significant fact in this account is that though he clearly is fallen, he still has access to God. That is what we must yet recognize about Satan: he has not been excluded from God's presence. Some books suggest that Satan is bound in hell, committed to a kind of furnace room in the universe, but these are distortions and far from the actual truth. Satan is granted access to heaven, and in that fact we have the first hint of the reason for the Book of Job; it is the first among many tremendous things this book has to say to us about the reasons for suffering.

Why do innocent, even righteous people, sometimes undergo terrible episodes of tragic injustice and suffering? This book will help us greatly with the answer to that question.

But there is a still deeper level of truth behind the Book of Job. Basically, it is given to us to reveal the relationship of Satan to God, that we may not be confused about the power of this vicious enemy against whom we all wrestle. Satan is not the equal of God. We do not have two gods, a good god and a bad god, struggling against each other. This book helps us to understand right from the start that God is in control of all things. All forces are at his command and nothing ever takes him by surprise. Nothing goes beyond his word and his will, including Satan.

This book will help us more than any other book in the Bible to catch a glimpse of the true greatness and majesty of God. We will see what we desperately need to see—that God is not just another man, great in power and authority, whom we can influence and command. God is not a heavenly bellboy, ready to run at our command, but he is in charge of all things, and he will always be in charge. If we are going to deal realistically with life, this is the way we must see him.

A Rigorous Test

We sometimes hear that the Book of Job is the record of a great battle between God and Satan, and that Job is caught in between. Although there

are aspects of this struggle in the book, it describes
a strange war in which one side must get permission
from the other before it attacks. What kind of a battle
is that? Can you imagine a German commander during World War II stepping up to General Patton,
saluting him, and saying, "Herr General, we would
like permission to bomb your troops, to destroy your
tanks, and to wreck all your plans!" I'm sure General
Patton's reply would have been unprintable. Yet this
is the situation in the Book of Job. Satan comes to
God and asks permission to attack Job. Now that is
not a battle, nor warfare; it is a test. What we must
see is that Job's faith becomes the subject of a very
rigorous test. Satan is the one who brings it about,
but God permits it.

The striking thing about this account is that it is
God who challenges Satan, not the other way around.
God says, "Satan, where have you been?" "Oh," says
Satan, "I've been here and there, looking over the
earth, trying to find somebody to attack." And God
says, "Have you taken a look at Job? There's a man
that I'm proud of!" God's own assessment of Job is
that there is none like him in all the earth. Job is
blameless and upright, i.e., he is well-balanced, and
he turns from evil as soon as he recognizes it. So
God asks Satan, "Have you tried Job?" Satan says,
"Well, I certainly have tried. I've looked that man
over very carefully, but I can't get near; you've got
him hedged in. I've tried every way I can to get
at Job, but you've got him so protected there's no
way I can get through."

Two things in particular emerge from this account—the satanic activity and the satanic philosophy. Satan's activity is to go up and down, looking
for somebody he can get at. This is in line with what

Peter tells us: "Your adversary [and here Peter uses the same term, the meaning of the name Satan] the devil prowls around like a roaring lion, seeking someone to devour" (1 Pet. 5:8). This is a tremendously helpful picture of some of the forces at work in our lives. A vicious, malicious enemy is looking for a chink in our armor.

In the letter to the Ephesians, Paul speaks also of giving the devil an opportunity. In chapter 4, verse 26, Paul says, "Be angry but do not sin; do not let the sun go down on your anger, and [therefore] give opportunity to the devil."

When do you give the devil an opportunity to get at you? When you hold a grudge, when you get mad at someone and refuse to forgive him, when you keep nursing and feeding your anger. The devil is watching and saying, "Ah, I've got a chance! I'll get him!" The suggestion here is that whoever reflects to some degree the devil's philosophy becomes available to his attack.

The devil's answer to God is, "You've protected Job, and that's why he serves you. But if you take away your protection, he'll curse you right to your face." According to Satan's philosophy, self-service is the fundamental law of life; "What's in it for me?" is the ultimate question for every human being. Put men in the right circumstances, where they have to choose between what is best for them and something else, and they will choose for themselves every time. Thus whoever begins to reflect the devil's philosophy becomes open to the devil's activity.

Now the Lord says to Satan, "Behold, all that he has is in your power; only upon himself do not put forth your hand." A third fact emerges in this account now. It is satanic limitation. God has set bound-

aries to Satan's activities. The impressive thing is
that although Satan is a rebel and would break the
rules if he could, there is no suggestion that he even
attempts to break forth from this limitation. There
is no possible way by which even Satan can violate
God's restriction. He has no power to do it and so
he abides by the rules. God is totally in control.

Now the rules of the test are clear. Job is to be
stripped of his possessions because Satan's argument
is that when they are taken away Job will deny God
right to his face. So God says to Satan, "All right,
we'll see. Go to it. He's in your power, but don't
touch his body."

The last part of chapter 1 gives us the terrible
results (vv. 13–15):

> Now there was a day when his sons and daughters were
> eating and drinking wine in their eldest brother's house;
> and there came a messenger to Job, and said, "The oxen
> were plowing and the asses feeding beside them; and the
> Sabeans fell upon them and took them, and slew the servants
> with the edge of the sword; and I alone have escaped to
> tell you."

Here came the first messenger of doom saying,
"Your oxen and asses are all gone. You know the
Sabeans, living over the hill? They came in a raid
and took them all, and slew the servants, and I am
the only one left, and have come to tell you."

> While he was yet speaking, there came another, and said,
> "The fire of God fell from heaven and burned up the sheep
> and the servants, and consumed them; and I alone have es-
> caped to tell you" (v. 16).

Perhaps this fire was some kind of lightning storm. More likely it was a volcanic eruption, in which brimstone and noxious gases sprayed the countryside, and the sheep and all the servants except this one were killed.

> While he was yet speaking, there came another, and said, "The Chaldeans formed three companies, and made a raid upon the camels and took them, and slew the servants with the edge of the sword; and I alone have escaped to tell you" (v. 17).

There goes Job's camels, the most prized possessions of the Arab world in terms of animals, taken in a raid by the Chaldeans.

> While he was yet speaking, there came another, and said, "Your sons and daughters were eating and drinking wine in their eldest brother's house; and behold, a great wind came across the wilderness, and struck the four corners of the house, and it fell upon the young people, and they are dead; and I alone have escaped to tell you" (v. 18).

What a terrible day! If you think you have been mistreated, look at this. The next time you get bad news I hope you will read through this chapter. The malignancy of Satan is revealed in that he struck to the full extent of his permission. He went right to the boundaries that God permitted him, and took away everything Job had. Satan did not ease the load, he did not stretch it out, he gave no time for preparation of heart and mind. One after the other, four times, the hammer fell, and every time Job's heart was crushed. And as a final blow, he lost all his sons and daughters.

Divine Permission

In this account we see that Satan is given power over natural forces. Some have misinterpreted this, saying that the devil is always the one who controls the wind and the waves. But I do not think that is necessarily true. Many of the Psalms speak of God's control and power in the natural world. We should remember here that Satan must always obtain divine permission to use these natural forces for his own ends.

When Jesus stilled the wind on the Sea of Galilee, he rebuked the wind and the waves. Now Jesus was not talking to air and water—he was talking to the forces behind them, the satanic power that was using these forces to stir up a storm. Evidently, judging from this account in the Book of Job, Satan had to receive permission from God the Father to bring that storm into being.

Whenever we read of the terrible destruction of hurricanes that come in various places in the world, we must understand that Satan, the god of this world, is at times given permission to bring these things about. I know that atheists often use that fact to present Christian teaching about the character of God in the worst possible light. They say, "Your Bible says that your God allows that to happen. What kind of a God have you got?"

I remember years ago reading a parody of the doxology:

Blame God from whom all cyclones blow,
Blame him, all creatures here below.
Blame him, who knocks down church and steeple,
Who sends the floods, and drowns the people.

The trouble with that is, there is a modicum of truth in it. It is God who has allowed it to happen. This is what makes our faith tremble and quail, and we come up with superficial answers to what is happening.

One Christian defense is to say, "Well, Satan is a kind of independent agent, and he does what he likes. God has given him areas in which he can operate, and has no control over him." But when you read an account of some public disaster, such as a great earthquake, a volcanic explosion, or even, as in this case, a raid by one enemy upon another, you must always read it with a realization that though Satan has been the instrument by which that was done, the will of God is also involved in it. Satan has demanded and obtained from God the power to bring that to pass.

This is one reason why the Book of Job is given to us, to show that there is a far deeper reason for God's permission of tragedy than the superficial answers we often give. This reason will be unfolded as we go on in this book. We will see that God is not, as Satan would love to have him painted, a cold impersonal God who does not really care for us, and who does not mind submitting us to tortures and indecencies and injustices. Rather, as James tells us, God is merciful and compassionate, and out of this book will emerge the revelation of the mercy and compassion of God.

No Complaints

Now we see Job's reaction (v. 20):

> Then Job arose, and rent his robe, and shaved his head, and fell upon the ground, and worshiped.

Job did not complain, he did not blame God, he did not get angry and upset and say, "Why should this happen to me? What have I done that all these things should suddenly come upon me?" C. S. Lewis once remarked when asked, "Why should the righteous suffer?" "Why not? They're the only ones who can handle it."

So Job's response is

"Naked I came from my mother's womb, and naked shall I return; the Lord gave, and the Lord has taken away; blessed be the name of the Lord" (v. 21).

He is saying, "Thank God for the times when I did have these things, and the enjoyment they gave me; the times with my children, and the blessings they brought into my life. Rather than complain about their loss, I recognize God's sovereign right to do with me as he will. If he gives me things, he has the right to take them away. All I can do is say 'Thank you' for having had them as long as I did." So we read,

In all this Job did not sin or charge God with wrong
(v. 22).

He has won the first round. It is clear that Satan's argument has been answered. Take away the possessions of a man like Job, and he still will not curse God to his face. He still loves God and follows him and serves him, and recognizes God's rights. It is a severe test and I wonder, how many of us would have passed it? But the test is not over—there is much worse yet to come. Before this book is through we will see levels of pride in Job of which he was totally unaware. We will begin to see what God is after in Job's life, and in ours, by this kind of testing.

Now you may be wondering, "What's going on behind the scenes about me? I wonder what Satan is saying about me now, and if he's asking permission to get me!" If that is what you are thinking, all I can say is, do not worry, live one day at a time. For one thing this book tells us is that if Satan had his way, every one of us would always be in this kind of difficulty. Satan would wreck us and hurt us and tear us apart all the time if he could—not because he is angry at us, but because he wants to get at God, whom we serve.

But God's protecting hand has been over us. If we have any degree of peace and enjoyment it is because the hand of God has been like a hedge about us, protecting us and giving us great and wonderful blessings. Therefore, the attitude of every human heart ought to be, "Thank God for what I've got! Thank God for where I am now. What the future may hold, only he knows." And if it holds some kind of testing like this, Paul has reminded us in 1 Corinthians, "God will not test you above what you are able to bear."

He knows what you can bear, and he will not put you to a test so severe it must destroy your faith. But there are implications in every test that go far beyond the superficial aspects of the situation. As this remarkable book unfolds, we will see some of the things that God brought to the attention of Job.

Our heavenly Father, we are grateful that we have so much blessing in our lives. How much your hand has given! How much it has poured into our life already, in terms of joy, pleasure, peace, relationship, warmth and love. We can only give thanks, Lord. And rather than complain about what we do not have, Lord, help our hearts to be filled with gratitude for what we have. Help us to know that your heart of love is watching over us, and protecting us from a vicious and evil being who would destroy us in a second if he could. Make us grateful for that. In Jesus' name, Amen.

2

The Pressure of Pain

Dr. Francis Schaeffer has said that the first argument of the gospel is not, as we often think, that Jesus died for our sins. Nor is it, as we are sometimes told, "God loves us, and has a wonderful plan for our lives." Dr. Schaeffer says that the first argument of the gospel is, "God is there." There is a God, and he is in control of life.

This is the great lesson of the Book of Job which we are faced with right from the beginning: the presence of God in the life of a man, even though he is going through severe trials. The trial itself proves the existence of God and man's relationship to him.

As we have already seen, Job is being subjected to a severe test. Satan has been permitted by God to take away all Job's possessions in an attempt to prove that if a man's possessions are taken away, he will curse God to his face. But Job has survived that first cycle of tests—tests that took away his wealth, his possessions, even his children. Job is left crushed and broken but, nevertheless, full of faith. The score is one to nothing in favor of Job against Satan.

Chapter 2 opens with another round in the test, and the first three verses tell us that God again initiates action against Job:

> Again there was a day when the sons of God came to present themselves before the Lord, and Satan also came among them to present himself before the Lord. And the Lord said to Satan, "Whence have you come?" Satan answered the Lord, "From going to and fro on the earth, and from walking up and down on it." And the Lord said to Satan, "Have you considered my servant Job, that there is none like him on the earth, a blameless and upright man, who fears God and turns away from evil? He still holds fast his integrity, although you moved me against him, to destroy him without cause."

This reads much like the first chapter where we have the same glimpse behind the scenes into the heavenlies, where God and Satan are holding a conversation about Job. As we move on in the Book of Job let us not forget these opening chapters, for they give us a heavenly view of earthly trials, and viewpoint makes a tremendous difference.

Here in this chapter we are given a viewpoint of Job and his suffering that Job himself is not permitted to have. We will not be permitted this viewpoint in the times of our own trial. We will not know either, what is going on behind the scenes in our lives when we come into pressures and trials. We will not know what has transpired between Satan and God about us, but the story of Job gives us this assurance that an agreement has been made and that we are being subjected to a test.

A Change in the Rules

The thing that is important here is that God initiates further testing of Job. God challenges Satan and says, "Well, what do you think of Job now? You moved me against him without a cause, and I allowed it to happen. But now what do you think? There is none like him on the earth. He is blameless and upright, and he turns away from evil. You haven't moved him an inch. What do you think now?" Satan replies by asking for a change in the rules:

> Then Satan answered the Lord, "Skin for skin! All that a man has he will give for his life. But put forth thy hand now, and touch his bone and his flesh, and he will curse thee to thy face." And the Lord said to Satan, "Behold, he is in your power; only spare his life" (vv. 4–6).

When Satan says "Skin for skin!" he is using basically the same argument that he used in the first chapter. His philosophy was (and is) that men are basically self-centered creatures. When you attack them directly they will give up their faith, their religion, anything, to save their comforts. But that argument has been fully answered. God has allowed Satan to test Job and though he has lost his family and all his wealth Job remains steadfast in his integrity, refusing to charge God with wrong.

It is really sobering to realize that the tests which come into our lives are aimed at getting us to curse God to his face, to tell him he is wrong, he does not keep his promises, he is not the kind of a God whom we have been told he is. You will probably recognize this fact: when you are under pressure the thing you want more than anything else is to cry out in protest to God that he is not keeping his promises. That is where Satan always aims. He has the same philosophy and the same objective today; he wants us to curse God, as he wanted Job to curse God.

But now Satan asks for a change in the rules. He says to God, "You didn't go far enough. You put a boundary about Job and said I couldn't touch his body. That's the problem. It's true that a man may give up his possessions, but one thing he will never give up is his health. You let me destroy his health, and he will give up his integrity and his faith."

"But put forth thy hand now, and touch his bone and his flesh, and he will curse thee to thy face." And the Lord said to Satan, "Behold, he is in your power; only spare his life."

Once again there is a divine limitation to the power of Satan, but this time God moves the boundaries closer. He says, "You can touch him, but do not destroy him. . . ."

When Satan uses the phrase, "touch his bone and his flesh," he asks for access to the total humanity of Job. We still use that phrase today, flesh and bone, to speak of our total humanity—not only our physical body, but our emotional life as well; not only our soul, but also our spirit. Satan is asking for access to this man Job, to touch him, body, soul and spirit— and he proceeds in that order. This constitutes the argument and basic assault recorded in the rest of the book of Job. Satan knows what he is after. He feels that if he can get at Job in every part of his being he can shake Job's faith and cause him to turn from his trust and confidence in God, to curse him to his face.

In a conversation with two young men on the Book of Job, I found they would not accept the story of Job as a historical event. I asked them why not. Their reply was, "If that story is true, then God is unconcerned about human life for it pictures God as ruthless; Job's whole family was taken from him. We can't accept that as a historical record."

I realized that they were struggling with the same feelings with which many people struggle today. They see God as nothing more than a man, who thinks and acts as a man and has no more rights than a man. If a man took life as ruthlessly as that, he would be justifiably charged with murder and cruelty. It does not occur to them that God cannot be charged with such cruelty because in his hand is the right of life. He determines the length of life for everyone. If Job's children had died from sickness these people would not charge God with ruthlessness and cruelty. But because they were taken suddenly, it seems unfair.

I remember clearly one occasion when my wife and I felt strongly the protests of many to the Book of Job. We received a phone call informing us that a beautiful young woman whom we had met not long before had been found dead. She and her husband, both Christians, were operating a Christian retreat and they had befriended our daughters who were living near by. The young woman and her husband were out for a walk beside a mountain stream. She sat down for a rest while he went ahead to climb a rock. When he came back, he found the body of his wife floating in the stream, drowned. Thus, suddenly, their five children were left motherless. Because they were such beautiful young people, and she was a very unusual mother, it hit us hard. Our hearts protested, "Why should this happen? What is God doing, taking a mother away from five children who need her desperately?"

But this is why we have the Book of Job. It shows us there are reasons and purposes in these trials and sufferings that we do not see. Job could not see what was going on behind the scenes, and neither can we. And yet God knows. He has a purpose for what he allows—a proper and right purpose that will end up manifesting more fully the love and compassion of his heart.

Boils and Recriminations

So Satan is given access to Job, and in the next section we see the physical test that follows:

> So Satan went forth from the presence of the Lord, and afflicted Job with loathsome sores from the sole of his foot to the crown of his head. And he took a potsherd with which to scrape himself, and sat among the ashes. Then his wife said to him, "Do you still hold fast your integrity? Curse God, and die" (vv. 7–9).

Here is the first attack on the body of Job. Some think it was leprosy; other scholars see it as a form of elephantiasis, which not only covered the body with running, putrefying sores, but also caused the members to swell up and become bloated and distorted. Whatever it was, it rendered Job a pitiful spectacle, a repulsive hulk of a man, swollen and disfigured and hurting.

In my early twenties I went through a siege of boils that lasted about two years. They came mostly one at a time, for which I was grateful. On one occasion I had two or three at once. Nothing is more painful, I think, than a boil, and it is the kind of pain that cannot easily be relieved. Day and night it throbs away. It was a severe test to my faith to have even that limited·trial.

But here is Job, totally covered with these agonizing sores. He was not only physically afflicted, but he was also painfully humiliated. He ends up sitting in the ashes, scraping the pus from his sores with a broken piece of pottery. To cap it all, the one to whom he ought to have been able to turn for emotional support turned against him. His wife said to him, "Do you still hold fast your integrity?" It is evident that her faith has crumbled under this attack. She no longer believes that God is loving, compassionate, and just. She sees this as proof (as many of us have done in times of trial) that God has forsaken his promises, that the Bible is not true.

How many times I have come to comfort people going through trials and had them say to me, "I tried these promises. I tried believing God—but it doesn't work." Have you ever said that? That is getting very close to what Satan was trying to get Job to do: "Curse God, and die." Job's wife is his instrument, just as Eve became the instrument to get at Adam in the Garden of Eden. So the assault upon Job's emotional life comes through his wife.

She advises him to do two things: "Give up your faith" (i.e. apostatize) "and curse God" (actually, in the Hebrew, the word is "bless" God, but it is properly translated "curse" because the word "bless" is dripping with sarcasm.) ". . . and die." She is clearly suggesting suicide: "It would be better for you to take your life than to go on like this." So poor Job, bound by physical pain, sits in humiliation with a disfigured body, and suffers from a sense of emotional abandonment by his mate.

I wonder if women fully understand how much their husbands depend on them for support in emotional crises. Husbands often draw emotional strength from their wives far more than either they or their wives realize. Here was a severe attack addressed to the very soul of Job, in which he felt even his wife abandoning him, advocating that he turn from his faith and renounce his God.

A Gentle Rebuke

But now in verse 10 we see the results of this second round of tests:

> But he said to her, "You speak as one of the foolish women would speak. Shall we receive good at the hand of God, and shall we not receive evil?" In all this Job did not sin with his lips.

Job's rebuke is a gentle one. He did not call her, "You foolish woman!" He said, "You speak as one of the foolish women." He is not attacking her; rather, he is suggesting that this is a temporary lapse of faith on her part and that for the moment she has begun to repeat the words of stupid, foolish women who have no knowledge of the grace and glory of God. In that gentle rebuke you can see something of the sturdiness and tenderness of Job's faith. In this great sentence he again reasserts the sovereignty of God: "Shall we receive good at the hand of God, and shall we not receive evil?" Job's wife had the philosophy that life ought to be pleasant and if it was not, there was no use living it. That philosophy is widespread in our own day, and a mounting suicide rate testifies to the broad acceptance of it.

But Job is given to show us that life is not to be lived on those terms. The reason we are here is not necessarily to have a good time. There are meaningful objectives to be attained in life, even when it all turns sour. When the pressure comes, when living is no longer fun, life is still worth living. A philosophy that wants to abandon everything as soon as things become unpleasant is a shallow, distorted view of life.

Job reaffirms that, "Shall we not take both good and evil from the hand of God?" We take God's joy and his pleasure, the pleasant things of life, with gladness and gratitude. If he chooses to send something that is difficult, shall we then abandon that gratitude and begin to curse him in protest, all because life is suddenly different than we thought it would be? God, in his grace and glory, does give us many, many hours of joy, and it is right for us to give thanks. But do not abandon that attitude when the time of pressure comes, for this is what Satan wants us to do. He wants us to complain and protest to God, to become upset and angry and resentful, to stop going to church, or to cease reading the Bible.

Well, Job has won again. The score is now two to nothing, in favor of Job. But Satan is not through. Remember that he obtained permission from God to assault this man in every area of his being. He has not only taken Job's children and all his possessions, but he has also taken away his health, and all the pleasure of his physical life. He has attacked not only his body but he has also assaulted Job's soul, making him feel abandoned by his wife.

The Final Stronghold

Satan now proceeds to attack the final stronghold: the spirit of Job, the ultimate reality of his life. In the closing verses of this chapter we see him beginning to move up his heavy artillery to attack the citadel of Job's faith. The big guns that he seeks to employ are rather unusual:

> Now when Job's three friends heard of all this evil that had come upon him, they came each from his own place, Eliphaz the Temanite, Bildad the Shuhite, and Zophar the Naamathite. They made an appointment together to come to condole with him and comfort him (v. 11).

We are now set for the major argument of this book. The supreme attack on the faith of Job comes not through his physical trials, but through an attack on his spiritual relationship with God himself. And it comes, ironically, through the hands of well-meaning friends. Here are misguided but sincere friends who want to help, and hope they are helping, but actually they are an instrument of Satan to assault the castle of Job's faith and almost cause it to collapse.

We will learn more about these men as we go through the arguments they bring forth. Evidently they had to come from distant places, and a good deal of time has probably elapsed during which Job has been suffering physically. Word had to come to his friends about Job's disaster and they had to agree together by sending messengers to one another to meet at an appointed time and visit Job. So weeks, if not months, have probably gone by while Job is subjected to this severe pressure upon his faith. When the friends arrive, they are utterly shocked at what they see:

> And when they saw him from afar, they did not recognize him; and they raised their voices and wept; and they rent their robes and sprinkled dust upon their heads toward heaven. And they sat with him on the ground seven days and seven nights, and no one spoke a word to him, for they saw that his suffering was very great (vv. 12, 13).

They can hardly believe their eyes! This monstrous, repulsive hulk of a man—could he really be their dear old friend Job? Could this creature, sitting huddled in a heap of ashes, scraping himself with a broken piece of pottery, swollen and disfigured, be the man they had known and loved? They are so shocked that their actions strongly suggest they think Job is on his deathbed. In effect, they hold a funeral service for him. These men do what was customary at funerals—raise their voices, mourn and weep. They tear their coats, sprinkle dust on their heads, and finally end up sitting on the ground around Job, observing him in silence for seven days.

He Deserves It!

Now while they were sitting there they were thinking. What they thought will come out in the arguments given in the next section of the book. It is enough for us to see at this point that while they were waiting in silence around Job they came to the conclusion that he was suffering under the hand of God for some terrible sin he must have committed—and that it was right for God to make him suffer this way. Their hearts, therefore, were hardening against Job. They had come to comfort him, but they were confronted with the feeling that many of us have had; there was not much they could say because in their heart of hearts they believed Job deserved what he was getting. The silence probably means that they were wondering how to begin, how to put their message in terms to which Job will listen.

As we go on we will hear Job's plaintive cry of protest against God, and we will read what these friends have to say as they try to explain to Job what he is going through. Much of our own philosophy will be reflected in what they say. But let us never forget that it is God who is bringing about this trial, and he has an aim in view. Because he does not tell us at this point what it is, we too must suffer through this with Job. We must feel to some degree what he is feeling, and sense the protest, the anguish, the emptiness of his life. Nevertheless, we must remember that there is an answer; God does have a reason, and it will be made clear as the book unfolds.

Sooner or later we all come to these times of trial and testing, for in some degree God visits them upon us all. If you are going through such a time this book will be of great help. But if you are not, be thankful that God has given us this book, and be thankful that, for the moment at least, he has chosen to maintain his protection, his loving care over you.

If Satan had his way, we would all perish. But God has guarded us and kept us. If he temporarily lifts his hand we have assurances everywhere in the Word of God that it will never be more than we can handle. Job proved that. It never was more than he could stand, although he thought it was. Sometimes this is the way we feel. We think God is going too far, pushing us too hard, but he never does; he is teaching us our limits. This is what the Book of Job will do for us as we go through it.

> *Our Father, we are sobered by this book. We see something of the blood and tears that life can confront us with, and of the ruthless pressures to which we can sometimes be subjected, and still be in your will and in your hand, guarded and guided by your love. Lord, we do not understand that, but that is because our understanding is so limited. We pray that as we go through this book we will have our eyes opened to the kind of God we deal with, and to the ways you work, and what the ultimate meaning will be in our own lives. Teach us now by your Spirit, in the name of Jesus our Lord. Amen.*

3

Is It Better to Die?

At this point in the Book of Job, Satan leads three of Job's friends to come and comfort him. When these friends arrive they are so shocked at what they see that they sit in silence for seven days before they can muster up enough courage to speak to Job about his troubles. Furthermore, they have begun to suspect that perhaps Job really deserves what he is going through. We will see how Satan uses this to increase Job's torment and anguish.

Chapter 3 begins with a dialogue between Job and his friends. The first thing we hear is a bitter lament from Job. Weeks have gone by since he was first afflicted with this painful disease, and God does not seem to explain what he is doing. Baffled and buffeted, tormented with physical misery, Job now opens his mouth with a tremendous cry in which he longs for death.

I do not know if you have ever felt that way, but there have been times when I wished I could have dropped out of the earthly scene entirely and gone home to heaven. I once received a card from a friend that referred to a trial my wife and I were going through. It said, "You may feel so very helpless now (which indeed you are for the most part) but I know when you are out there and the crutches one by one are stripped from you, God's words and his love will stand before you irresistibly and constantly until Jesus becomes your only alternative. Otherwise, death would be the only seemingly logical relief." That is where we find Job now, crying out for death, cursing the day he was born.

Let the Day Perish

In this chapter he asks three poignant questions. The first one is, "Why was I ever born?" Listen to the eloquent way he expresses it:

After this Job opened his mouth and cursed the day of his birth. And Job said:

"Let the day perish wherein I was born,
    and the night which said,
    'A man-child is conceived.'
Let that day be darkness!
    May God above not seek it,
    nor shine upon it.
Let gloom and deep darkness claim it.
    Let clouds dwell upon it;
    let the blackness of the day terrify it.
That night—let thick darkness seize it!
    let it not rejoice among the days of the year,
    let it not come into the number of the months.
Yea, let that night be barren;
    let no joyful cry be heard in it.
Let those curse it who curse the day,
    who are skilled to rouse up Leviathan.

Let the stars of its dawn be dark;
    let it hope for light, but have none,
    nor see the eyelids of the morning;
because it did not shut the doors of my mother's womb,
    nor hide trouble from my eyes" (vv. 1–10).

This book is written in marvelous poetry. Here
Job is saying that he hopes his birthday will be forgotten: "May the anniversary of it be ignored. Let it
be a day that is darkened, let no one rejoice in it.
Let it be a day of cursing instead of blessing." All
he has enjoyed in the past seems of no value in the
fact of this tremendous anguish. You can see the
pressure is increasing, and Job is beginning to break
and crumble under it.

I do not think anything is harder for us to bear
than unexplained trouble. If we could see some reason for what we have to go through we could endure
it much more easily. But when trouble seems to be
pointless and nothing is accomplished by it, it is a
terrible strain upon the soul.

In verse 11 through 19, Job's second question is,
"Having been born, why didn't I die at birth?"

"Why did I not die at birth,
    come forth from the womb and expire?
Why did the knees receive me?
    Or why the breasts, that I should suck?"

"My life has been totally meaningless," Job says. "It
would have been better to have died when I was
born." Then he goes on to give us his view of death,
a view that is much more primitive than what we
have in the New Testament. It is a more natural
view, widely held by many people who do not know
anything at all about the Bible.

"For then I should have lain down and been quiet;
  I should have slept; then I should have been at rest,
with kings and counselors of the earth
  who rebuilt ruins for themselves,
or with princes who had gold,
  who filled their houses with silver.
Or why was I not as a hidden untimely birth,
    [an abortion]
  as infants that never see the light?
There the wicked cease from troubling,
  and there the weary are at rest.
There the prisoners are at ease together;
  they hear not the voice of the taskmaster.
The small and the great are there,
  and the slave is free from his master" (vv. 12–19).

Job views death as a time of rest, a period of solitude and quiet after the tumult and trouble of life. I think many people see death that way. In the play, "Our Town," there is a vivid scene in the cemetery where the dead are talking among themselves. To them, death is the absence of all opportunity to fellowship with those left alive; all is quiet and peaceful. These verses indicate that Job's understanding of life after death needs to be enlightened a great deal, and that is one of the reasons why this suffering comes into his life. At the end of the book Job's view of death is quite different than it is here at the beginning.

Job's third question is, "Why can't I die now?" His questions have a logical sequence "Why was I born? But, having been born, why didn't I die when I came out of the womb? And since that didn't happen, why can't I die now?" In verses 20 to 26 he asks:

"Why is light given to him that is in misery,
  and life to the bitter in soul,

who long for death, but it comes not,
    and dig for it more than for hid treasures;
who rejoice exceedingly,
    and are glad, when they find the grave?
Why is light given to a man whose way is hid,
    whom God has hedged in?
For my sighing comes as my bread,
    and my groanings are poured out like water.
For the thing that I fear comes upon me,
    and what I dread befalls me.
I am not at ease, nor am I quiet;
    I have no rest; but trouble comes." [keeps coming]

Job's argument is, "What's the purpose of my life? Of what use is a life that is so filled with misery that you can do nothing but suffer and feel anguish? My life produces only fear and trouble, so it would be better to end it now." Many people feel that way. I do not think Job is thinking of suicide—he is asking God to end his days. There is no purpose to life, he says, when it is not enjoyable.

At this point we get the first of the replies of the three friends of Job. They are named Eliphaz, Bildad, and Zophar. These friends all come with the same solution to the problem, but they approach it in three distinct ways, according to their personalities. They might well be nicknamed: "Eliphaz the Eloquent," "Bildad the Brutal," and "Zophar the Zealous."

Follow Your Own Advice

Eliphaz is evidently the oldest, for there is a smoothness about him, and a courtesy (at least at the beginning) that indicates he has learned how to say unpleasant things in gracious ways. Bildad is brutal and plainspoken. He lays it on Job and does not care what the effect is. Zophar is compassionate and emotional, but he speaks with a great deal of force, trying to move Job. Eliphaz's first argument breaks down into six main points, and when you hear what he has to say you will know what these three friends will be saying all through the rest of the book. He starts out by saying to Job, in effect, "Follow your own advice."

"If one ventures a word with you, will you be offended?
  [Notice the courtesy with which he starts!]
 Yet who can keep from speaking?
Behold, you have instructed many,
 and you have upheld him who was stumbling,
 and you have made firm the feeble knees,
But now it has come to you, and you are impatient;
 it touches you, and you are dismayed.
Is not your fear of God your confidence,
 and the integrity of your ways your hope?" (4:2–6)

Basically Eliphaz is saying, "Job you have been a counselor to many people, and you have been able to put your finger on their problem and help them to deal with it. You delivered them, you found the key to what was troubling them and helped them to face up to it. Now your turn has come; follow your own advice and you will be relieved." Then Eliphaz goes on to state just what the problem is, and in verses 7 to 11 we learn his basic principle of life:

"Think now, who that was innocent ever perished?
 Or where were the upright cut off?
As I have seen, those who plow iniquity
 and sow trouble reap the same.
By the breath of God they perish,
 and by the blast of his anger they are consumed.

The roar of the lion, the voice of the fierce lion,
  the teeth of the young lions, are broken.
The strong lion perishes for lack of prey,
  and the whelps of the lioness are scattered."

Eliphaz uses a family of lions to describe the natural strength of human beings—it appears to be strong, but in God's judging hand, it is broken. His argument is that the righteous are never punished; only the unrighteous suffer. "Where did you ever see an innocent man perish?" he asks Job. "Where did you ever see an unrighteous man succeed?" His argument is, clearly, that Job's problem is caused by his own sin, something he is hiding. "There is something wrong, Job. If you will only admit it you'll be all right."

I remember years ago picking up a Christian magazine that specialized in attacking men in public ministry. The editor of the magazine said of Dr. Billy Graham, who had just had a certain illness, that it was a judgment of God on him because he associated with the wrong kinds of people. But what fascinated me was that in the next issue the editor announced that he himself had fallen down a flight of stairs and broken his leg! His explanation of it was that Satan was attacking him, trying to stop his God-given ministry! This is so characteristic of humanity. We all see clearly that the suffering of others is caused by their sin, but our suffering is always caused by something else.

Unbalanced Theology

Eliphaz goes on to tell Job that if he will fear God and admit his sin, things will be all right. He breaks down his message into two parts. First, he says, he learned this truth in a vision that came to him at night. It is a rather spooky passage:

> "Now a word was brought to me stealthily,
>   my ear received the whisper of it.
> Amid thoughts from visions of the night,
>   when deep sleep falls on men,
> dread came upon me, and trembling,
>   which made all my bones shake.
> A spirit glided past my face;
>   the hair of my flesh stood up.
> It stood still,
>   but I could not discern its appearance.
> A form was before my eyes;
>   there was silence, then I heard a voice:
> 'Can mortal man be righteous before God?
>   Can a man be pure before his Maker?
> Even in his servants he puts no trust,
>   and his angels he charges with error;
> how much more those who dwell in houses of clay,
>   whose foundation is in the dust,
>   who are crushed before the moth.
> Between morning and evening they are destroyed;
>   they perish for ever without any regarding it.
> If their tent-cord is plucked up within them,
>   do they not die, and that without wisdom?' " (vv. 12–21).

That is an argument based upon the fact that infinite justice rules the universe. Eliphaz sees God as a God of holiness and purity, so spotless that even the angels of God stand defiled before him. What chance would a man have to stand before him and claim to be sinless? In a sense, that is good theology. As we will see before the end of the book, it was a problem Job was really facing; he did not understand all his own heart, and he so confesses this at the end. But the trouble with Eliphaz's argument is that he thinks there has to be some known but hidden sin which Job is unwilling to confess. Eliphaz sees God only as a God of justice. He sees nothing of love and compassion and forgiveness, or of discipline and training from the Father's hand. So, because of his unbalanced theology, even though what he says is true it becomes false in its application.

In this way, much error creeps into the way some people use Scripture. We can quote truths from the Bible, but when we try to apply them out of a false premise, we end up wrong. Some people make a habit of going around with a Bible, quoting verses to others. They end up virtually beating others over the head with these verses. Charles Spurgeon, the great English preacher, used to speak about "preachers who went about with a theological revolver in their ecclesiastical trousers." This was Eliphaz's approach.

In chapter 5, verses 1 to 7, Eliphaz argues that trouble comes only from sin:

> "Call now; is there any one who will answer you?
>   To which of the holy ones will you turn?
> Surely vexation kills the fool,
>   and jealousy slays the simple."

"That is what is wrong; you are vexed and jealous, and that is why you have trouble!"

> "I have seen the fool taking root [apparently prospering],
>   but suddenly I cursed his dwelling [it all fell apart].
> His sons are far from safety.
>   they are crushed in the gate,
>   and there is no one to deliver them."

What a low blow! That is a hidden reference to the calamity that befell all Job's children in one day.

Eliphaz is suggesting that such things happen only because there is something wrong in Job's life.

"His harvest the hungry eat,
   and he takes it even out of thorns;
   and the thirsty pant after his wealth.
For affliction does not come from the dust,
   nor does trouble sprout from the ground;
but man is born to trouble
   as the sparks fly upward."

"Trouble comes from sin," says Eliphaz. "If you've got trouble, sin has to be the reason."

Get It Out in the Open

In the next division, verses 8 through 16, he suggests to Job that there is no use playing games with God because God knows too much.

"As for me, I would seek God,
   and to God would I commit my cause;
who does great things and unsearchable,
   marvelous things without number:
he gives rain upon the earth
   and sends waters upon the fields;
he sets on high those who are lowly,
   and those who mourn are lifted to safety.
He frustrates the devices of the crafty,
   so that their hands achieve no success.
He takes the wise in their own craftiness;
   and the schemes of the wily are brought to a quick end.
They meet with darkness in the daytime,
   and grope at noonday as in the night.
But he saves the fatherless from their mouth,
   the needy from the hand of the mighty.
So the poor have hope,
   and injustice shuts her mouth."

God is in control, Eliphaz argues, and he is so clever and wise that you cannot deceive him. "You can't hide from him, Job. He'll trap you, he'll uncover your sin. You might as well get it out in the open!" Eliphaz closes with a section which says, in effect, "Just give up, and God will bless you."

> "Behold, happy is the man whom God reproves;
>   therefore despise not the chastening of the Almighty.
> For he wounds, but he binds up;
>   he smites, but his hands heal.
> He will deliver you from six troubles;
>   In seven there shall no evil touch you.
> In famine he will redeem you from death,
>   and in war from the power of the sword.
> You shall be hid from the scourge of the tongue,
>   and shall not fear destruction when it comes.
> At destruction and famine you shall laugh,
>   and shall not fear the beasts of the earth.
> For you shall be in league with the stones of the field,
>   and the beasts of the field shall be at peace with you.
> You shall know that your tent is safe,
>   and you shall inspect your fold and miss nothing.
> You shall know also that your descendants shall be many,
>   and your offspring as the grass of the earth.
> You shall come to your grave in ripe old age,
>   as a shock of grain comes up to the threshing floor in its
>   season.
> Lo, this we have searched out; it is true.
>   Hear, and know it for your good" (vv. 17–27).

Eliphaz argues that if Job will cast himself on God's mercy, he will forgive him and restore him and everything will be fine. Job can be confident that he will be protected and kept, even to a ripe old age. Now of course the truth is, that is not what happens. Anyone who has lived a few years at all knows it is possible to find godly people who are not protected, who still go through times of trial and peril and suffering. Though this sounds like good theology, it does not take in all the facts. This story is given to us so that we might learn to correct our theology, and to understand that there are deeper reasons for suffering than sin.

A Right to Complain

Job's reply to this comes in chapters 6 and 7. It is divided into two sections. In chapter 6 Job rebukes his friends, speaking to all three of them. (Probably there were others present, listening to all this—a silent audience, except for a certain young man who comes in at the end of the book.) In chapter 7 Job addresses his complaint to God. There are three parts to each chapter. First, Job says he has a right to complain.

Then Job answered:
"O that my vexation were weighed,
　and all my calamity laid in the balances!
For then it would be heavier than the sand of the sea;
　therefore my words have been rash" (6:1–3).

He admits he has been speaking very strongly, but he says, "If you were where I am, you'd understand. My sorrow is so terrible it gives me a good reason to complain. . . .

"For the arrows of the Almighty are in me;
　my spirit drinks their poison;
　the terrors of God are arrayed against me.
Does the wild ass bray when he has grass,
　or the ox low over his fodder?

Can that which is tasteless be eaten without salt,
   or is there any taste in the slime of the purslane?
My appetite refuses to touch them;
   they are as food that is loathsome to me" (6:4–6).

"You never hear an animal complain," Job says,
"when he is well fed and taken care of. That's why
I am complaining. You cannot take that which is
tasteless and loathsome without trying to improve
it with salt, or something. So I have a right to complain. It helps me to bear my troubles." Many people
talk that way; many feel that if God sends them tribulation, they have a right to tribulate! Then Job speaks
of his inability to bear more:

"O that I might have my request,
   and that God would grant my desire;
that·it would please God to crush me,
   that he would let loose his hand and cut me off!
This would be my consolation;
   I would even exult in pain unsparing;
   for I have not denied the words of the Holy One.
What is my strength, that I should wait?
   And what is my end, that I should be patient?
Is my strength the strength of stones,
   or is my flesh bronze?
In truth I have no help in me,
   and any resource is driven from me" (6:8–13).

"I have no strength to handle this. What does God
think I am made of, stone or bronze, that he subjects
me to all this?" Have you ever felt that way? Have
you ever said, "Lord, you promised that you would
not tempt me above that which I'm able to bear,
and Lord, we went by that point weeks ago!" But
God knows us better than we know ourselves. He
knows how much we can take. So Job's cry goes unanswered.

Then Job rebukes his friends, expressing his irritation at their lack of understanding (vv. 14–21):

> "He who withholds kindness from a friend
>   forsakes the fear of the Almighty.
> My brethren are treacherous as a torrent-bed,
>   as freshets that pass away,
> which are dark with ice,
>   and where the snow hides itself.
> In time of heat they disappear;
>   when it is hot, they vanish from their place.
> The caravans turn aside from their course;
>   they go up into the waste, and perish.
> The caravans of Tema look,
>   the travelers of Sheba hope.
> They are disappointed because they were confident;
>   they come thither and are confounded.
> Such you have now become to me. . . ."

Job says, "You friends are like a mountain brook that is full of water in the wintertime when nobody needs it. But when the hot summer sun comes out, and you long for the refreshing of the water, it is nothing but a dry, gravel-filled stream bed. Even the caravans of camels looking for water for refreshment find nothing there. You said you came to comfort me, and all you've given me is trouble. You only rebuke me." Job is obviously irritated at these friends (vv. 22, 23):

> "Have I said, 'Make me a gift'?
>   Or, 'From your wealth offer a bribe for me'?
> Or, 'Deliver me from the adversary's hand'?
>   Or, 'Ransom me from the hand of oppressors'?"

"Did I ask you to help me? I didn't send for you. You came to comfort me and instead you rebuke me!"

"Teach me, and I will be silent;
     make me understand how I have erred.
How forceful are honest words!
     But what does reproof from you reprove?
Do you think that you can reprove words,
     when the speech of a despairing man is wind?
You would even cast lots over the fatherless,
     and bargain over your friend.
          [You'd even beat your grandmother!]
But now, be pleased to look at me:
     for I will not lie to your face" (vv. 24–28).

Job is simply saying, "If there is something wrong, then tell me, for I don't know what it is." His dilemma is that he knows God is doing this to him, but he cannot find a reason. He knows there is nothing in his life that he has not already confessed and dealt with. While he is not claiming to be sinless, he is saying that he has handled whatever sin he has been aware of, so what else is there?

Then he turns to God, and complains about the hardness of his present experience (7:1–6):

"Has not man a hard service upon earth,
     and are not his days like the days of a hireling?
Like a slave who longs for the shadow,
     and like a hireling who looks for his wages,
so I am allotted months of emptiness,
     and nights of misery are apportioned to me.
When I lie down I say, 'When shall I arise?'
     But the night is long,
     and I am full of tossing till the dawn.
My flesh is clothed with worms and dirt;
     my skin hardens, then breaks out afresh.
My days are swifter than a weaver's shuttle,
     and come to their end without hope."

How painful are the days of this troubled man! We become concerned when we get a pimple on our face, but Job was covered with boils! Then he complains about the hopelessness of the future:

> "Remember that my life is a breath;
>   my eye will never again see good.
> The eye of him who sees me will behold me no more;
>   while their eyes are upon me, I shall be gone.
> As the cloud fades and vanishes,
>   so he who goes down to Sheol does not come up;
> he returns no more to his house,
>   nor does his place know him any more" (vv. 7–10).

I Will Complain!

He has given up. He thinks he will never see any relief, that he will go on like this to the end. And out of that meaningless suffering and hopeless darkness, he cries out in honest despair:

> "Therefore I will not restrain my mouth;
>   I will speak in the anguish of my spirit;
>   I will complain in the bitterness of my soul.
> Am I the sea, or a sea monster,
>   that thou settest a guard over me?
> When I say, 'My bed will comfort me,
>   my couch will ease my complaint,'
> then thou dost scare me with dreams
>   and terrify me with visions,
> so that I would choose strangling
>   and death rather than my bones.
> I loathe my life; I would not live forever.
>   Let me alone, for my days are a breath.
> What is man, that thou dost make so much of him,
>   and that thou dost set thy mind upon him,
> dost visit him every morning,
>   and test him every moment?
> How long wilt thou not look away from me,
>   nor let me alone till I swallow my spittle?
> If I sin, what do I do to thee, thou watcher of men?
>   Why hast thou made me thy mark?
>   Why have I become a burden to thee?

Why dost thou not pardon my transgression
  and take away my iniquity?
For now I shall lie in the earth;
  thou wilt seek me, but I shall not be" (vv. 11–21).

Have you ever felt like this? "Lord, leave me alone,
I've had enough! Why are you so intent on making
life miserable for me? Why don't you just let me
go?" Now, even at this point in the book, we must
constantly remember that in every time of trial there
are two purposes in view: Satan has his purpose, and
God has his.

Satan's purpose here was to use the pain of Job's
illness to afflict his body; to use the priggish, well-
intentioned comfort of his friends to irritate his soul;
and to use the silence of God to assault his spirit
and to break his faith. But God's purpose is to teach
Job some truths he never knew before, to deepen
his theology and help understand God and himself
much better. God's purpose was to answer Satan
before the principalities and powers of the whole
universe, and to prove him wrong in his philosophy
of life. God's purpose was also to provide a demonstration for all sufferers in the ages to follow that
God knows what he is doing.

*Our Father, thank you for the sufferings of Job. What marvel-
ous lessons they teach us about our own lives and our own
sufferings. Help us to view them in the light of the revelation
of this book, and to know that we know more truth than
Job knew, and we have far less reason to give up than he
did. Grant to us, Lord, strength to stand in the midst of
pressure, through Jesus Christ our Lord. Amen.*

4

The Folly of Platitudes

The three men who came to comfort Job prove to be the severest trial he has yet to bear. The eloquent and lofty arguments of Eliphaz only leave Job angry and irritated, crying out for enlightenment from his friends and relief from his pain. Now the second of Job's three friends takes up the attack. He is Bildad the Shuhite, but I have called him "Bildad the Brutal." His short discourse opens by attempting to use logic with Job:

Then Bildad the Shuhite answered:
"How long will you say these things,
　and the words of your mouth be a great wind?
Does God pervert justice?
　Or does the Almighty pervert the right?
If your children have sinned against him,
　he has delivered them into the power of their
　transgression" (8:1–4).

Bildad's style is to ask questions in an effort to focus everything into a logical framework. He is the cold, intellectual thinker who debates the issue at the level of the mind. His first question, "Can God do wrong?" is a good question to ask, and the basis of much philosophy. Of course, the logical answer is, "No, God cannot do wrong." After all, ideas of what is wrong and what is right are based upon the very nature and character of God himself. Rightness is being like God; wrongness is being unlike God. So to ask this question is to ask, "Can God be unlike himself?" The answer is no, God cannot be unlike himself. God cannot do wrong.

So Bildad moves on from that basic premise to draw a logical conclusion for Job: "If your children have sinned against him, he has delivered them into the power of their transgression." "When your children died, Job, on that tragic day when the tornado blew down the house and killed them all, you can only properly conclude it was because they did something terribly wrong." Bildad is following through the line of argument that all three of these friends pursue; God punishes all wrong, therefore any tragedy is the result of some definite though perhaps hidden sin.

Bildad goes on to argue that God will respond to repentance, and he summons the past experience of the fathers to confirm this:

"For inquire, I pray you, of bygone ages,
 and consider what the fathers have found;
For we are but of yesterday, and know nothing,
 for our days on earth are a shadow" (vv. 8, 9).

There is much truth in what these men say to Job. In fact, it is difficult to find anything specifically wrong in what they say. Bildad is simply reminding

Job that the experience of the past confirms the fact that God blesses those who turn to him, and that he rebukes and punishes those who turn away.

Then Bildad supports his argument further with various common sayings of the day (vv. 11–13):

> "Can papyrus grow where there is no marsh?
>   Can reeds flourish where there is no water?
> While yet in flower and not cut down,
>   they wither before any other plant.
> Such are the paths of all who forget God;
>   the hope of the godless man shall perish."

His argument is clearly that man, by nature, must have God's blessing in order to prosper. If he does not have it, if he has done something to cut himself off from the blessing of God, then he will simply wither like a reed without water. Then he points out how God always cuts off those who seem to prosper because of evil in their midst, and he closes with an exhortation to Job to repent:

> "Behold, God will not reject a blameless man,
>   nor take the hand of evildoers.
> He will yet fill your mouth with laughter,
>   and your lips with shouting.
> Those who hate you will be clothed with shame,
>   and the tent of the wicked will be no more" (vv. 20–22).

This is a heartfelt and earnest exhortation to Job to own up to whatever it is he is hiding from them and from God, and perhaps from himself.

When you read these arguments, you have to ask, "What is wrong with this? It sounds so true and right." It is an argument you hear repeated many times today. What Bildad says is true and logical, and supported by plausible argument both from the experience of the past and from the testimony of Scripture. What, then, is wrong?

It's What's Left Out That Hurts

At the end of the book, God appears and says that Job has been saying the right things and that the friends are wrong in what they say. But at this point we have to ask, "What is wrong with this?" The answer, of course, is that it is said in the wrong spirit, and what they leave out makes it wrong.

There are three things wrong with their approaches. First, they answer Job's words without trying to find out what lies behind them. They zero in on what he says, without understanding his agony. Job has already admitted that he speaks rashly, but it is because of the unceasing torment he is going through. Any of us who have gone through deep, unrelenting pain knows how this can try the spirit to the utmost, and we become testy and sharp. Because Job says certain things that sound extreme, his friends leap upon his words and try to analyze them without identifying with his hurt.

This is a common problem in marriage. Husbands often are coldly analytical when their wives are pressured, or weary, or frightened about something. Husbands hear only the words and try to analyze them—and nothing can destroy a woman faster. The problem is that there is no identification with the hurt.

The second thing is that these friends' theology is incomplete. They always speak with the utmost confidence that what they are saying is the final word on the subject. There is no apparent understanding that perhaps there were aspects of God and dimensions to his Word which they had not yet seen. As many of us do today, they judge only on the basis of a rigid theology that takes note of certain aspects of truth, but ignores others.

The third thing wrong with these friends is that they never pray with Job. They never ask God for help to open their minds and to illuminate their understanding so that they can help their friend. The book is filled with prayers, but they are all the prayers of Job, crying out to God in the midst of his sufferings. His friends never seem to feel the need for further illumination on the subject. Yet you cannot find much wrong with their arguments. What a testimony to us of the need to speak cautiously when we deal with the deep hurts and problems of life.

Job's Dilemma

In chapters 9 and 10 we have Job's reply to Bildad. In chapter 9 he sets forth the difficulty he has with God, and he opens with a statement of his dilemma:

Then Job answered:
"Truly I know that it is so:
 But how can a man be just before God?
If one wished to contend with him,
 one could not answer him once in a thousand times"
(vv. 1–3).

We must carefully understand what Job is saying here. He also has an inadequate theology; he accepts the principle that trouble comes only because of sin. He would have analyzed another's problems along the same line before his own trials began. But in the long dark hours of searching his own heart he has not been able to put his finger upon any sin with which he has not already dealt. So his dilemma is, "I'm not aware of sin in myself, yet the trouble is there; therefore, the problem must lie in God."

But Job has no way to examine God, and he goes on to state this in very eloquent terms. First, he says that God's wisdom is beyond man:

"He is wise in heart, and mighty in strength
—who has hardened himself against him, and succeeded?—
he who removes mountains, and they know it not,
    when he overturns them in his anger;
who shakes the earth out of its place,
    and its pillars tremble;
who commands the sun, and it does not rise;
    who seals up the stars;
who alone stretched out the heavens,
    and trampled the waves of the sea;
who made the Bear and Orion,
    the Pleiades and the chambers of the south;
who does great things beyond understanding,
    and marvelous things without number" (vv. 4–10).

"How can you get hold of a God like that to debate with him the issues that are causing the hurts of life?" Job asks.

In verses 11 and 12 he recognizes God's invisibility:

"Lo, he passes by me, and I see him not;
    he moves on, but I do not perceive him.
Behold, he snatches away; who can hinder him?
    who will say to him 'What doest thou'?"

In verses 13 and 21 we have a marvelous statement of the sovereign activities of God in history.

"God will not turn back his anger [he does not change his
mind];
beneath him bowed the helpers of Rahab [Egypt].
How then can I answer him,
choosing my words with him?
Though I am innocent, I cannot answer him;
I must appeal for mercy to my accuser.
If I summoned him and he answered me,
I would not believe that he was listening to my voice.
For he crushes me with a tempest,
and multiplies my wounds without cause;
he will not let me get my breath,
but fills me with bitterness.
If it is a contest of strength, behold him [obviously the win-
ner]:
If it is a matter of justice, who can summon him?
[Who can judge the judge?]
Though I am innocent, my own mouth would condemn me;
though I am blameless, he would prove me perverse.
I am blameless; I regard not myself;
I loathe my life."

First Ray of Light

In verses 22 and 24 he goes on to describe how
life becomes incomprehensible where there is no
understanding God. The reference point is gone, or
uncertain, or vague; you cannot make sense of anything in life. And in verses 25 through 31 we see
the effect this has on Job; he is filled with bewilder-
ment, fear, and despair. But then in verses 32
through 35, out of the deep darkness that surrounds
this suffering saint, a ray of light breaks through. It
is the first break in Job's gloom. He says of God:

"For he is not a man, as I am, that I might answer him,
that we should come to trial together."

Then comes the awareness of what is missing:

> "There is no umpire between us,
>   who might lay his hand upon us both.
> Let him take his rod away from me,
>   and let not dread of him terrify me.
> Then I would speak without fear of him,
>   for I am not so in myself."

"What is needed is a mediator, an arbitrator who understands us both, and who can bring us together," Job says. For the first time in this book we begin to see why God is putting Job through this protracted trial. For now Job begins to feel, deep in his bones, the terrible gulf between man and God that must be bridged by another. We who live in the full light of the New Testament know that he is calling out of a deeply felt need for just such a mediator as Jesus himself. Job is laying the foundation in his own understanding for the tremendous revelation of the New Testament: God becomes a man. God takes our place, lives as we live, feels as we feel, and solves the great problem between us and God, bringing God and man together. For the first time in Job we begin to sense what God is driving at. There is a verse in Psalm 119 that says:

> It is good for me that I was afflicted,
>   that I might learn thy statutes (v. 71).

You can learn theology out of a book, you can study it and get it clear in your mind, but until you go through the hurts and difficulties and trials of life, you never really understand what the truth is. It takes suffering to get a clear vision of what God is saying to us.

In chapter 10 the darkness closes in again around

Job. Once again his torment drives him to prayer, and this chapter is breathed out before God, in the presence of his friends. There are two things Job asks in this prayer. In verse 2 he says,

. . . "let me know why thou dost contend against me."

Then in verse 20 he cries to God, "Let me alone, that I may find a little comfort." So his prayer consists of these two cries, "Let me know, or else let me alone; one or the other!" Anyone who has gone through suffering knows that this is often our feeling.

Examining the Possibilities

In the first 17 verses of chapter 10, Job is searching for answers, examining all the possibilities that might explain why he is going through this torment. It is apparent that they reflect the questions every sufferer faces when he is going through a difficult time. In verse 3 Job asks:

"Does it seem good to thee to oppress,
  to despise the work of thy hands
  and favor the designs of the wicked?"

That is, "Do you get some kind of pleasure out of this? Is that why you put me through this?" I do not think Job is being sarcastic. I think he is really asking, "Is God that kind of a being, that this pleases him? If that is the explanation, at least I am contributing to the pleasure of God by going through this!" Then he asks in verses 4 through 7:

"Hast thou eyes of flesh?
  Dost thou see as a man sees?

Are thy days as the days of man,
      or thy years as man's years,
that thou dost seek out my iniquity
      and search for my sin,
although thou knowest that I am not guilty,
      and there is none to deliver out of thy hand?"

He is asking God, "Do you somehow limit yourself to man's circumstances and capabilities? Is that why you put me through this? Despite your wisdom and knowledge and might, do you limit yourself to our knowledge, put yourself where we are, and let yourself act and think only like a man? Is that what is behind this?" Here we have certain intimations of the Incarnation, the great underlying truth of the New Testament, that God will limit himself and become a man, putting himself in our place, that he might fully understand how we feel.

In verses 8 through 13, Job argues, "You made me, you formed me, and now you tear me apart. Is that a reasonable thing to do? You who put me together are now destroying me. Is that logical, is that right?" Then in verses 14 through 17 he asks, "What can I do? What recourse do I have? How can I please you or change in such a way as to alleviate this suffering?"

"If I sin, thou dost mark me . . .
If I am wicked, woe to me!
      If I am righteous, I cannot lift up my head, . . .
And if I lift myself up, thou dost hunt me like a lion . . ."
                                                        (vv. 14).

And he closes (v. 17):

"Thou dost renew thy witnesses against me,
      and increase thy vexation toward me;
thou dost bring fresh hosts against me."

"What can I do? Where can I turn?" Every argument that has ever occurred to a suffering saint is brought out here in the Book of Job. In fact, every nuance of suffering, whether mental or physical, is explored to its utmost throughout this book. All the tormenting questions are asked. All the haunting dilemmas are faced. Anyone going through suffering will find that Job has felt whatever he has, and has articulated it eloquently. The questions are not answered at this point. They will be answered before we are through, but in a way we could never anticipate.

Now, because of the silence of God, Job closes this chapter by crying out, "Let me alone! Life is useless; death is but darkness. Whatever it is, anything is better than this. Let me alone."

A Scorching Rebuke

In chapter 11, Zophar the Naamathite (let us call him "Zophar the Zealous") moves up to bat, and he opens with a scorching rebuke to what he sees as Job's sinful folly:

Then Zophar the Naamathite answered:
"Should a multitude of words go unanswered,
    and a man full of talk be vindicated?
Should your babble silence men,
    and when you mock, shall no one shame you?
For you say, 'My doctrine is pure,
    and I am clean in God's eyes.'
But oh, that God would speak,
    and open his lips to you,
and that he would tell you the secrets of wisdom!
    For he is manifold in understanding.
Know then that God exacts of you less than your guilt de-
    serves" (vv. 1–6).

One can almost see Zophar shaking his fist in righteous indignation in Job's face. He accuses Job of wordiness, of foolishness, of mockery, of self-righteous smugness. He says that Job's punishment is richly deserved; he is only getting what is coming to him, and not even all of that. What a sweetheart this man is! He goes on in verses 7 through 12 to describe Job's stupid ignorance, in contrast to God's deep wisdom and inscrutable ways:

"Can you find out the deep things of God?
    Can you find out the limit of the Almighty?
It is higher than heaven—what can you do?
    Deeper than Sheol—what can you know?
Its measure is longer than the earth,
    and broader than the sea.
If he passes through, and imprisons,
    and calls to judgment, who can hinder him?
For he knows worthless men;
        [guess who Zophar has in mind!]
    when he sees iniquity, will he not consider it?
But a stupid man will get understanding
    when a wild ass's colt is born a man."

That is, it will never happen. "Anybody as stupid as you, Job, will never get any help." He lays it on, heavy and hard. Then he closes with a vivid description of the shining possibilities that are ahead, if Job will only repent:

"If you set your heart aright, . . .
If iniquity is in your hand, . . .
Surely then you will lift up your face without blemish;
    you will be secure, . . .
You will forget your misery; . . .
And your life will be brighter than the noonday; . . .

And you will have confidence, . . .
    you will be protected . . .
You will lie down, and none will make you afraid; . . ."
                                            (vv. 13–19).

Then a sharp word of warning at the end,

"But the eyes of the wicked will fall;
    all ways of escape will be lost to them,
and their hope is to breathe their last" (v. 20).

Once again there is no identifying with Job's hurt, no empathy. This man just lays it on him with ruthless zeal. He sees only the cold, analytical logic of the situation. Zophar, of course, speaks with a great deal of passion and force, but there is no intimation that he is offering understanding help.

This is the difference between mere theology and the counsel of a man taught by the Spirit. Theology can be clear and proper and correct, but it is all in the head. When you are dealing with the hurting problems of life, you must add a deeper dimension—the compassion that Jesus manifested, the sympathy that identified with the hurt and opened the door of the spirit to receive what light might be given through the words.

The first round of dialog ends with Job's sarcastic defense in chapters 12 through 14. The first part is Job's answers to his friends; the second is his prayer before God. (We will leave that prayer for the next chapter.) Now Job speaks to his friends:

Then Job answered:
"No doubt you are the people,
    and wisdom will die with you" (12:1, 2).

We know exactly how he felt; these men have all the answers! Job says, "When you pass from the scene, there will be nothing left. You know it all." From verse 3 on to the end of the chapter, he points out that they deal with elementary truths, things anybody could know:

> "But I have understanding as well as you;
> I am not inferior to you.
>   Who does not know such things as these?" (v. 13).

"You haven't helped me. Anyone knows this; you haven't added anything to my knowledge." Then he begins to detail it:

> "I am a laughingstock to my friends;
>   I, who called upon God and he answered me,
> a just and blameless man, am a laughingstock" (v. 4).

Why? Because—

> "In the thought of one who is at ease
>   there is contempt for misfortune . . ." (v. 5).

"You don't understand because you've never been here. You haven't felt what I feel." (How familiar that argument is!) And then Job says, "You haven't faced all the facts" (v. 6):

> "The tents of robbers are at peace,
>   and those who provoke God are secure,
> who bring their god in their hand."

"You tell me God always punishes unrighteousness, but look around you. There are idolaters who openly bring their idols in their hands. There are robbers living at peace; God is not punishing them. Life itself testifies that you are wrong."

In verses 7 through 12 he says nature confirms that God deals as he pleases; there is no way of predicting his actions:

> "But ask the beasts, and they will teach you;
>   the birds of the air, and they will tell you;
> or the plants of the earth, and they will teach you;
>   and the fish of the sea will declare to you . . .
> In his hand is the life of every living thing,
>   and the breath of all mankind."

Finally, in a beautifully moving passage filled with great passion, Job shows that he understands God fully as well as they do (vv. 13–25).

A Plea for Silence

In chapter 13 Job continues his defense before these men. He says their words have not helped; their silence would help more:

> "Lo, my eye has seen all this,
>   my ear has heard and understood it.
> What you know, I also know;
> I am not inferior to you.
> But I would speak to the Almighty,
>   and I desire to argue my case with God.
> As for you, you whitewash with lies;
>   worthless physicians are you all.
> Oh that you would keep silent,
>   and it would be your wisdom!" (vv. 1–5).

In verses 6 through 12 he tells them that if God judges him, he will also judge them; if God overwhelms him, he will overwhelm them also. They

are in exactly the same boat. So his final plea is to
let him alone, that he might come before God himself and debate this whole matter (vv. 13–19):

> "Let me have silence, and I will speak,
>   and let come on me what may.
> I will take my flesh in my teeth,
>   and put my life in my hand.
> Behold, he will slay me; I have no hope;
>   yet I will defend my ways to his face."

Verse 15 is translated quite differently in the Authorized Version. This is the famous passage often quoted
from Job:
    "Though he slay me, yet will I trust in him."
It is a great cry of hope and trust, but it is not really
what Job said. What he said, I think, is best translated
in the Revised Standard Version:

> "Behold, he will slay me; I have no hope;
>   yet I will defend my ways to his face."

He is determined, Job says, to defend himself, but
he expresses one bit of hope in verse 16:

> "This will be my salvation,
>   that a godless man shall not come before him."

"If I am really godless, I will not get a chance to
come before him. But if he will give me a chance,
I have my case all prepared. And the very fact that
he will listen to me indicates that at least I have a
chance." So he concludes:

> "Listen carefully to my words,
>   and let my declaration be in your ears.

Behold, I have prepared my case;
I know that I shall be vindicated.
Who is there that will contend with me?
For then I would be silent and die" (vv. 17–19).

Beginning at verse 20 through the rest of the chapter and on through chapter 14, Job presents the case that he has prepared before God, and he tells us what he would say if he could talk to God. But here he simply makes a plea that his "comforters" stop arguing and listen to him, and help him by their silence.

Surely, if nothing else, this Book of Job should help us to be careful in our approach to the suffering of others, so that we do not add to it. These friends of Job are so rigid in their theology, so blind to the great dimensions of God, that neither they nor Job understand they are only increasing the torment of this poor man. This is why Scripture exhorts us to "Weep with those who weep, and rejoice with those who rejoice."

Our Father, help us to understand more of your great nature, the majesty and glory of your being, the compassion of your heart, and the wisdom that prompts you to put us through times of difficulty and yet offers to support us through them, without fail. Lord, help us to learn from this book, that we might better handle that which comes to us. We ask in Jesus' name, Amen.

5

Help from On High

Men who are waiting for trial often haunt prison libraries to study law books for their own defense. Sometimes they become such experts in law that they actually assume the presentation of their own case before the jury. Job is like that, for chapter 13 describes how, through long hours of anguish, he is planning what he would say if God ever gave him a chance.

He has four major points he wants to make. The first is a plea for certain conditions that he feels must be met before he is able to stand and talk to God:

"Who is there that will contend with me?
   For then I would be silent and die.
Only grant two things to me,
   then I will not hide myself from thy face:
withdraw thy hand far from me,
   and let not dread of thee terrify me.
Then call, and I will answer;
   or let me speak, and do thou reply to me" (vv. 19–21).

C. S. Lewis has well said that to argue with God is to argue with the very power that makes it possible to argue at all. Job senses this; he knows he must have mercy from God before he can even stand before him, so he asks for two conditions to be granted him. First, he asks that God will lift the pain and anguish he is going through so that he does not have to speak out of constant torment. Second, he asks God to so veil his presence that Job will not be terrified by the awesomeness of a mighty God. It is a vivid revelation of the sense of God that Job has, even in his hour of anguish.

One thing Job never loses is his consciousness of the character of God. Even though he wonders at what God is doing, and feels that he is being mistreated in many ways, he retains a vivid sense of the majesty of God. Here he asks that he be delivered from fear so that he might present his case.

A Right to Know

The next division contains Job's cry for knowledge. He needs further information before he can go on:

"How many are my iniquities and my sins?
Make me know my transgression and my sin" (v. 23).

It is universally recognized in any court of law that a prisoner has the right to know the charges placed against him. Job does not know what his sin is, although he has searched his heart. His theology— along with that of his friends—tells him that punishment and suffering come because of sin. But what sin? That is what he cannot answer. So he cries out, "What have I done? How have I offended?"

Then he protests the silence of God, and God's apparent anger against him:

"Why dost thou hide thy face,
and count me as thy enemy?
Wilt thou frighten a driven leaf
and pursue dry chaff?
For thou writest bitter things against me,
and makest me inherit the iniquities of my youth.
Thou puttest my feet in the stocks,
and watchest all my paths;
thou settest a bound to the soles of my feet" (vv. 24–27).

The only thing that occurs to Job that may be an explanation of his unrelenting pain is that God is going back and picking up the sins of his past, even the sins of his youth, despite the fact that he had offered sacrifices for them according to God's program.

Then in chapter 14, in two marvelously moving passages, Job brings out the helplessness and the hopelessness of man before God. First, he is helpless to control his affairs:

"Man that is born of a woman is of few days,
and full of trouble.
He comes forth like a flower, and withers;
he flees like a shadow, and continues not" (vv. 1, 2).

And yet God judges this limited, helpless man, who is a victim of circumstances, for things he cannot help:

"Since his days are determined,
and the number of his months is with thee,
and thou hast appointed his bounds . . ." (v. 5).

"What can man do? He is a victim of what happens to him." This is the expression of Job's heart, and many have felt this way. "I can't help it that I was born into this situation, subjected to these pressures, and these circumstances. What can I do?"

The latter part of the chapter expresses very eloquently man's sense of hopelessness; most of us have said, "Oh, I wish I could go back and live it through again—at least some of it. If I could go back, knowing what I know now, I could clear up so many of my mistakes. Give me another chance, God, now that I have learned what I need to know." That is a universal feeling, and Job feels it. Yet he expresses his consciousness that this is impossible:

"For there is hope for a tree,
  if it be cut down, that it will sprout again,
  and that its shoots will not cease. . . .
"But man dies, and is laid low;
  man breathes his last, and where is he?
As waters fail from a lake,
  and a river wastes away and dries up,
so man lies down and rises not again;
  till the heavens are no more. . . ." (vv. 7, 10–12).

That is Job's pessimistic view of life. Here we are dealing with a great problem that everyone faces. We often have a distorted view of this life, which Job expresses in eloquent terms. He goes on in the next passage, verses 13 and 14, to cry out for a kind of purgatory after life:

"Oh that thou wouldest hide me in Sheol,
  that thou wouldest conceal me until thy wrath be past,
that thou wouldest appoint me a set time, and remember
  me!"

And then he asks again:

"If a man die, shall he live again?"

And the hope that something could be worked out causes him to say,

"All the days of my service I would wait,
till my release should come."

No Hope of Purgatory

Those words vividly describe the joy it would be to stand before God with God's wrath already past. Job is not describing this because he thinks it is possible for him. He is voicing the inarticulate longings of the human heart to be freed from guilt—guilt that we do not always feel we can help. This has given rise to a hope for a purgatory after death, where we can pay for some of our sins and the rest of them are set aside, so that at last we can stand accepted before God. Chapter 14 closes with a graphic description of the helplessness of man:

"But the mountain falls and crumbles away,
     and the rock is removed from its place;
the waters wear away the stones;
     the torrents wash away the soil of the earth;
     so thou destroyest the hope of man.
Thou prevailest for ever against him, and he passes;
     thou changest his countenance, and sendest him away.
His sons come to honor, and he does not know it;
     they are brought low, and he perceived it not.
He feels only the pain of his own body,
     and he mourns only for himself" (vv. 18–22).

This poetic expression describes what is wrong with our view of life. Job is looking at life as a natural man. He sees it as the world sees it, centered only on our present existence. This life is the important thing, and the reason we were brought into existence is to make something out of this present experience—we never get another chance. How frequently we are reminded of this on television: "You only go around once. Live life with gusto." This is one of the major reasons why couples break up, sometimes after 25 or 30 years of marriage. People begin to feel the force of this argument and they truly believe it. They think the only thing to do, if there is to be any pleasure or enjoyment in life, is to seize the present moment. "I have not been able to get it together in all this time, so I'm going to leave and start over." Many a marriage has broken on that rock.

But God is teaching Job that this is a faulty view of life. This present human existence is but school time, a time of preparation for the real life that lies ahead. Compare Job's view of life with the revelation of the New Testament as to what lies beyond death and a startling contrast is evident. There Christians look forward to something so beautiful and glorious breaking upon them that they can hardly wait to seize it! But in Job we see again the concept that everything must be done now.

The Friends Attack

With Job's response round one is complete; the three friends have all had a chance at Job. Now his friends gird up their loins, sharpen their spears, and come at him again. In the first six verses of chapter 15, Eliphaz the Temanite charges Job with presumptuous words:

> "Should a wise man answer with windy knowledge,
>   and fill himself with the east wind?

Should he argue in unprofitable talk,
　or in words with which he can do no good?
But you are doing away with the fear of God,
　and hindering meditation before God.
For your own iniquity teaches your mouth,
　and you choose the tongue of the crafty.
Your own mouth condemns you, and not I;
　and your own lips testify against you!" (vv. 2–6).

Eliphaz started out very courteously, but now he has dropped his courtesy and is thrusting deeply. He next accuses Job of pretentious claims:

"Are you the first man that was born?
　Or were you brought forth before the hills?
Have you listened in the council of God?
　And do you limit wisdom to yourself?
What do you know that we do not know?
　What do you understand that is not clear to us?"
　　　　　　　　　　　　　　　　　　　(vv. 7–9).

"We have the same sources of knowledge as you, Job. Why do you put us down and think yourself so smart?" Then he returns, as all the friends do, to their narrow and worn-out theology:

"What is man, that he can be clean?
　Or he that is born of a woman, that he can be righteous?
Behold, God puts no trust in his holy ones,
　and the heavens are not clean in his sight;
how much less one who is abominable and corrupt,
　a man who drinks iniquity like water?" (vv. 14–16).

Of course, Eliphaz has Job in mind here, "one who is abominable and corrupt, a man who drinks iniquity like water." Again, it is not that his theology is wrong. Eliphaz is pointing out the general nature of the depravity of man, the Fall and its effects upon human life. He rightly says that there is no one who is clean, no one who is righteous before God. But what he fails to do is to point out to Job, specifically, what it is that he has done. How can you deal with evil if you do not know what it is? The great revelation that God is seeking to help Job understand is the nature of his corrupt heart. But God never charges him with fault until Job begins to see what is wrong. These men come accusing him of every ugly thing in the book, though they had no proof whatsoever. Job's life gives the lie to all their charges. As a matter of fact, they too are guilty of the very things that they set before Job because they are part of the human race. Eliphaz is a man born of woman, so he is guilty along with Job, but we never hear a word of self-condemnation from him.

Eliphaz goes on, in a long passage, to argue again from experience. He goes back over all the past and says, "My thesis is true, everything proves it: God will not let a man get by with wickedness. The wicked are going to be punished. Therefore, if you are being punished you must be wicked!" He says in verses 34 and 35:

> "The company of the godless is barren,
>   and fire consumes the tents of bribery,
> They conceive mischief and bring forth evil
>   and their heart prepares deceit."

It is the same old tired thrust at Job: he must be guilty of some terrible sin.

In chapters 16 and 17, Job answers. He does not know what to say, but he is trying to be honest. The great thing about Job is that he is no hypocrite; he never tries to cover over or set his case in a better light—he simply blurts out all the hurt and anguish of his heart as best he can. He also rebukes these men for their misunderstanding.

> Then Job answered:
> "I have heard many such things;
>   miserable comforters are you all.
> Shall windy words have an end?
>   Or what provokes you that you answer?
> I also could speak as you do,
>   if you were in my place;
> I could join words together against you,
>   and shake my head at you.
> I could strengthen you with my mouth,
>   and the solace of my lips would assuage your pain"
>   (16:1–5).

Sarcastic words, coming from a tortured man. We can see from this that Satan is still there in the background, using these friends as channels for what the apostle Paul calls "the fiery darts of the wicked one," the accusations of the accuser of the brethren. Let us beware lest we become a channel for Satan's accusations against someone who is suffering as Job is suffering here.

God Is to Blame

Job goes on to state the facts as he understands them. First he says, "All I can conclude from what I am suffering is that God must hate me." Verses 7 through 9 tell us:

> "Surely now God has worn me out;
>   he has made desolate all my company.
> And he has shriveled me up. . . .
> He has torn me in his wrath, and hated me;
>   he has gnashed his teeth at me. . . .

Job goes on to show how even the people around him have rejected him, and how God is behind that:

> "Men have gaped at me with their mouth,
>   they have struck me insolently upon the cheek,
> they mass themselves together against me.
> God gives me up to the ungodly,
>   and casts me into the hands of the wicked.
> I was at ease, and he broke me asunder;
>   he seized me by the neck and dashed me to pieces;
> he set me up as his target,
>   his archers surround me . . ." (vv. 10–13).

Though Job charges God with all that is wrong in his life, God is wonderfully patient. He does not reply against Job, nor does he strike him down in anger. Job is certainly not the highest example of faith in the Scriptures. Men like Paul suffered extremely, as did Job. We think, too, of that silent sufferer in the Garden of Gethsemane, who, "when he was reviled, reviled not again, but committed himself unto him who judges righteously." How much higher is that level of response than what we see in the Book of Job! But Job is the example for us of how difficult it is for our natural view of life to be shattered. God sometimes has to translate theology into painful experience before we really begin to grasp what he is trying to say. Job ends by protesting his innocence again:

> "My face is red with weeping,
>   and on my eyelids is deep darkness;
> although there is no violence in my hands,
>   and my prayer is pure" (vv. 16, 17).

Then once again, as we have seen already, breaking through into Job's consciousness is a dim reflection of what God is trying to show him:

"O earth, cover not my blood,
    and let my cry find no resting place.
Even now, behold, my witness is in heaven,
    and he that vouches for me is on high" (vv. 18, 19).

Despite the charges Job makes against God (that this is all coming from his hand), faith emerges at this point to say that God must also supply the answer—God alone can explain what is happening to him. Job's faith lays hold of that great fact to give him some brief comfort in his agony. Almost everyone who is going through a time of struggle and trial asks the same basic question Job asks. The answer given most often in Scripture is that God has sent trial to wean us from dependence on people and to find our resource in God himself. God must separate us from the supports that frequently sustain us in hours of crisis in order that we may learn how fully able he is to keep us. So the truth gradually dawns upon Job that only God himself can answer the searching questions of his heart.

Chapter 17 presents Job's prayer that God will set him free. He prays for relief, but largely from his friends! He has had enough of them. He also expresses his need for defense: in verses 3 to 6 he describes the effects of his suffering upon others, especially these men; and then he challenges them in verse 10:

"But you, come on again, all of you,
    and I shall not find a wise man among you."

He has heard all their arguments and he knows they do not help, so in the final part of the chapter he sinks back again into the darkness of despair:

"My days are past, my plans are broken off,
    the desires of my heart."

In chapter 18 we have Bildad's defensive retort. It reflects the same line of argument as before. Bildad is the logician, the coldly analytical intellectual. He is angry that Job does not answer him in kindly fashion, and that Job has accused him of being unkind in his approach:

Then Bildad the Shuhite answered:
"How long will you hunt for words?
    Consider, and then we will speak.
Why are we counted as cattle?
    Why are we stupid in your sight?" (vv. 1–3).

Bildad goes on, from verse 5 to the end of the chapter, to set forth again the narrow, rigid dogma of his theology: If you are suffering, you must have sinned. I once heard a man described as "an evangelical crab." That is the only fitting term for Bildad the Shuhite.

Chapter 19 gives us a piteous plea of Job. First, he describes his feelings about his friends:

"How long will you torment me,
    and break me in pieces with words?
These ten times you have cast reproach upon me;
    are you not ashamed to wrong me?" (vv. 1–3).

Then in verses 7 through 12 he describes again his bafflement at what is happening to him:

"Behold, I cry out 'Violence!' but I am not answered;
    I call aloud, but there is no justice.
He has walled up my ways, so that I cannot pass. . . .

He has stripped from me my glory . . . (v. 9).
He breaks me down on every side" (v. 10).

In verses 13 through 19 we have a vivid description of the isolation he feels, coming from the hand of God:

"He has put my brethren far from me,
    and my acquaintances are wholly estranged from me.
My kinsfolk and my close friends have failed me;
    the guests in my house have forgotten me;
my maidservants count me as a stranger;
    I have become an alien in their eyes.
I call to my servant, but he gives me no answer;
    I must beseech him with my mouth.
I am repulsive to my wife,
    Loathsome to the sons of my own mother.
Even young children despise me;
    when I rise they talk against me.
All my intimate friends abhor me, . . ."

Surely nothing is harder to bear than the rejection of those who should understand. Job is feeling the terrible pain of this, as well as his physical pain. But in the midst of the darkness, when it is blackest and gloomiest, one of those amazing rays of light breaks through again. Elisabeth Elliot has written a book called *A Slow and Certain Light.* That is descriptive of what Job is experiencing here, for he cries, in verses 23 and 24:

"Oh that my words were written!
    Oh that they were inscribed in a book!
Oh that with an iron pen and lead
    they were graven in the rock for ever!"

How little he understood that these words would be literally fulfilled.

Then suddenly he sees a ray of hope,

"For I know that my Redeemer lives,
  and at last he will stand upon the earth;
and after my skin has been thus destroyed,
  then in my flesh I shall see God,
whom I shall see on my side [i.e., for myself],
  and my eyes shall behold, and not another" (vv. 25–27).

In response to that vision of faith, he cries.

"My heart faints within me!"

This is one of the great cries of faith in the Old Testament, one of the earliest intimations of the resurrection of the body found in the Word of God. Slowly, through the anguish and gloom of this man's heart, born out of the passion and the pathos he feels, comes the dawning realization that God is working out a great and mighty purpose, and that someday God himself (whom Job has never failed to see as a God of great majesty and power) will be visibly present before men. God will come himself, and vindicate all that he has done. This passage is a marvelous glance ahead, by faith, to the incarnation of Jesus. Job calls him "My Redeemer [i.e., my vindicator], the one related to me, who nevertheless will defend me and vindicate all that has happened to me."

Surrounded by Mystery

The study of the Book of Job helps us to understand that life is basically a mystery. We are surrounded with enigma. We cannot comprehend it all; it is painted on too large a canvas; it is too great and involved for us to grasp. Job is gradually learning, in the midst of his pain, to trust the God who is there; to believe that he will supply the answers he seeks, and that he is working out his purpose in line with his love.

I once heard Elisabeth Elliot describe her first widowhood. Her husband was slain, along with four companions, in the jungles of Ecuador at the hands of savages. She spent thirteen years as a widow, and then married a gracious and wonderful man with whom she was very happy. Then he died of cancer. She said, "I have spent six-sevenths of my life single, though I have been married twice. I did not choose the gift of widowhood, but I accepted it as the sphere in which I am to live to the glory of God."

That is what Job is gradually learning. God is working out a purpose. It is not related to specific sin although, as we will see before the book is over, Job learns much more about the depravity of his own nature. But now he ends his discourse by warning his friends to be careful about judging him:

> "If you say, 'How we will pursue him!'
>   and, 'The root of the matter is found in him';
> be afraid of the sword,
>   for wrath brings the punishment of the sword,
> that you may know there is a judgment" (vv. 28, 29).

Some time ago I ran across these words by an unknown poet. They wrap up in beautiful fashion the lesson of the Book of Job to this point:

> When God wants to drill a man,
> And thrill a man,
> And skill a man;
> When God wants to mold a man
> To play the noblest part,
> When he yearns with all his heart
> To create so great and bold a man

That all the world shall be amazed,
Watch his methods, watch his ways—

How he ruthlessly perfects
Whom he royally elects.
How he hammers him and hurts him,
And with mighty blows, converts him
Into trial shapes of clay
Which only God understands,

While his tortured heart is crying,
And he lifts beseeching hands.
How he bends but never breaks
When his good he undertakes.
How he uses
Whom he chooses,
And with every purpose, fuses him,
By every act, induces him
To try his splendor out.
God knows what he's about!

That is the message of Job to us. Some of you may be going through pain, suffering, disappointment and anguish, and you are crying out, as Job did, "Why? What have I done? Where does it all fit together?" Job's answer to us is, "God knows what he's about." One of these days all the answers will come in. In the meantime, rest in confidence that he knows what he is doing with you.

Thank you, our Father, for this reassurance to us who are going through far less than Job went through, with much greater light. Help us to cling to that light, and not charge you with injustice, as Job did, for we have no excuse, such as he had. Help us to accept, Lord, what is happening to us as your hand works out vast and wonderful patterns in our lives. We ask in Jesus' name, Amen.

6

Why Doesn't God Intervene?

One of the great benefits of the Book of Job is the glimpses we get in Job's three friends of what is called Pharisaism. Of course the Pharisaical party did not surface until many centuries after Job was written and in the New Testament the Pharisees became the primary enemies of our Lord. Pharisaism is always orthodoxy without godliness. It is an appearance of being orthodox, correct in theology, and outwardly righteous in behavior, but actually it represents a distortion of Christian truth.

The three men who were assaulting Job represent three varying styles of Pharisaism. As we read them we can recognize many of our own attitudes. Pharisaism is one of the most deadly enemies of truth today. In many ways the modern church has fallen into it, exhibiting a kind of outward rightness but inward wrongness. So as we hear these men we can perhaps recognize features about ourselves that need correction.

Zophar, the one whom we call "Zophar the Zealous," represents the type of Pharisaism that speaks with impassioned words and strong outbursts of feeling. He tries to carry his argument by the force of eloquence, especially in chapter 20, his last appearance in the book:

> Then Zophar the Naamathite answered:
> "Therefore my thoughts answer me,
>   because of my haste within me.
> I hear censure which insults me,
>   and out of my understanding a spirit answers me"
> (vv. 1, 2).

This man seems to be greatly insulted by the fact that Job does not accept the argument that sin is always judged by God, and therefore suffering is a sign that you have sinned. He confesses that he is both impatient in his speech and insulted in his spirit. It is because of this that he speaks with a great deal of passion to Job. His final argument is essentially nothing but repetition of what he has already said: the wicked are always punished. In verses 4 through 11, he argues that the prosperity of the wicked is always short. He says in verse 5, "The joy of the godless [is] but for a moment." Then in verses 12 through 18 he describes the punishment of the wicked as being very certain—there is no way to avoid it. Though the wicked seek to do so, and even revel in their prosperity, God will certainly bring judgment upon them. Now Zophar means that the wicked, the unrighteous, and the ungodly—those who ignore God—cannot, even in this present life, escape his judgment. God will get them sooner or later, while they are yet alive.

In verses 19 through 22 Zophar describes the

wicked as doing things that are clearly apparent; their evil comes out in the open. Obviously he is suggesting that because Job has gone through this time of torment, with these awful boils breaking out upon him, his evil too is coming into the open. Then he describes the terrible fate of the wicked (v. 23–29):

> "To fill his belly to the full
>   God will send his fierce anger into him,
>   and rain it upon him as his food.
> He will flee from an iron weapon;
>   a bronze arrow will strike him through.
>
> Utter darkness is laid up for his treasures . . .
>   (v. 26).
>
> The heavens will reveal his iniquity,
>   and the earth will rise up against him" (v. 27).

He closes with these words:

> "This is the wicked man's portion from God,
>   the heritage decreed for him by God" (v. 29).

In chapter 21 appears Job's very reasoned reply. There are times when Job speaks rather testily, even sharply, to his friends, and at other times, perhaps when the pain is not as intense, he is able to speak more calmly and dispassionately. Here in chapter 21 he makes a careful attempt to answer these arguments. He begins with an appeal for a hearing.

> Then Job answered:
> "Listen carefully to my words,
>   and let this be your consolation.
> Bear with me, and I will speak,
>   and after I have spoken, mock on.

As for me, is my complaint against man?
　　Why should I not be impatient?
Look at me, and be appalled,
　　and lay your hand upon your mouth [i.e., with astonishment].
When I think of it I am dismayed,
　　and shuddering seizes my flesh" (vv. 1–6).

Basically he is saying here, "If you can't help me, at least listen to me; that can be your consolation to me. You're trying to console me, and it's not helping a bit, but if you would listen to what I have to say, that would be some help from you. It is God who is my problem," he suggests; "not man, but God. I don't understand him." Then he says, "it is my condition, my pain and anguish, that forces me so to search and try to come to answers."

With that as an introduction, he now examines the argument that punishment is always the result of sin.

In verses 7 through 13 he says that the facts contradict what these friends say. In fact, the entire life of the wicked is often an untroubled one.

"Why do the wicked live,
　　reach old age, and grow mighty in power?
Their children are established in their presence,
　　and their offspring before their eyes.
Their houses are safe from fear,
　　and no rod of God is upon them.
Their bull breeds without fail;
　　their cow calves, and does not cast her calf.
They send forth their little ones like a flock,
　　and their children dance.
They sing to the tambourine and the lyre,
　　and rejoice to the sound of the pipe.
They spend their days in prosperity,
　　and in peace they go down to Sheol."

Their whole lives are lived, Job argues, and nothing ever seems to trouble them. They are outwardly and openly wicked, and yet they are happy, their families grow up well, and they seem to be free from difficulty. Many of us have felt this way. We see those who we think ought to be under the judgment of God but they are not; they seem to be untroubled. We are faced with the question of the fairness of God.

No Profit in Prayer

His second argument is that they even defy God, and still they prosper:

> "They say to God, 'Depart from us!
>   We do not desire the knowledge of thy ways.
> What is the Almighty, that we should serve him?
>   And what profit do we get if we pray to him?'
> Behold, is not their prosperity in their hand?
>   The counsel of the wicked is far from me" (vv. 14–16).

"I do not agree with this," he says, "but that is what they actually say. They defy God; they ask him to get out of their lives; they resist him; and God lets it be. Nothing ever happens to them; they seem to live untroubled lives, and God does not strike them down."

He goes on to point out that God's judgment is very infrequent:

> "How often is it that the lamp of the wicked is put out?
>   That their calamity comes upon them?
>   That God distributes pains in his anger?
> That they are like straw before the wind,
>   and like chaff that the storm carries away?" (vv. 17, 18).

It is very seldom that the wicked get their comeuppance in this life, he argues. Then he says that God's judgment is frequently delayed (v. 19–21), and finally, God's judgment is very uneven:

"Will any teach God knowledge,
  seeing that he judges those that are on high?
One dies in full prosperity,
  being wholly at ease and secure,
his body full of fat
and the marrow of his bones moist.
Another dies in bitterness of soul,
  never having tasted of good.
They lie down alike in the dust,
  and the worms cover them" (vv. 22–26).

Life seems to be unfair. There is a basic injustice at the root of things, and this is what causes many people to reject the claims of Christians about a loving, faithful, just and holy God. You often hear the question raised, "If there is a good God why does he let this kind of thing happen?" Job is raising the same question. He says to these pious, respectable friends, "Your arguments do not square with the facts. You say God always visits wrath upon the wicked. What about these wicked people who live without pain? God never does a thing to them. What about the fact that he treats people unfairly? Folks who seem to deserve nothing but the grace of God, who are loving, gentle, kind people, have endless problems, and die forsaken. And some who are selfish and cruel and self-centered are able to live without struggle. What about this?"

Then he turns to examine his friends, and points out the falseness of their friendship:

> "Behold, I know your thoughts,
>   and your schemes to wrong me.
> For you say, 'Where is the house of the prince?
>   Where is the tent in which the wicked dwelt?'"
>   (vv. 27, 28).

They were referring, of course, to Job. He says, "I know you're thinking that I am a good example of the truth of your argument because God has taken away my wealth, my family, my possessions. You're saying to yourself, 'Ah! Where is all the wealth of this man? Here is proof right here that what we say is true.'" Though they were not saying this quite as baldly, Job says, "I know what you are thinking, your hidden surmisings. I know also your unsupported convictions." In verses 29 through 33 he asks:

> "Have you not asked those who travel the roads,
>   and do you not accept their testimony
> that the wicked man is spared in the day of calamity,
>   that he is rescued in the day of wrath?
> Who declares his way to his face,
>   and who requites him for what he has done?
> When he is borne to the grave,
>   watch is kept over his tomb.
> The clods of the valley are sweet to him;
>   all men follow after him,
>   and those who go before him are innumerable."

He tells the friends, "If you'll just inquire around among the traveling salesmen, the people who get around and see life, you'll find that they support what I'm saying. It's not just true around here—it is true everywhere. The wicked live above the law, and nobody says to them that they're doing wrong. When they die, their graves are adorned and guarded and God does nothing about their wickedness." So he says at last:

"How then will you comfort me with empty nothings?
There is nothing left of your answers but falsehood"
(v. 34).

Experience Has the Advantage

If you intend to argue with Job you had better get your arguments well in hand. This man is able to see through the error of logic in the position of these friends. They have a theology that does not square with experience, and that is where the problem lies. These friends represent people—and there are many around today—who put God into a box. They have what they think is a clear understanding of all the ways of God and they can even predict how he is going to act. But when he acts in unexpected ways they have no way of handling it. It is their creed they have faith in, and not God himself. Job's creed has been demolished by his experiences. He has had to toss his theology in the wastebasket because it does not fit what he is going through. Someone has well said that a man with a true experience is never at the mercy of a man with an argument. These men are unable to answer Job because his experience rings true.

This answer of Job concludes the second round of addresses, and in chapter 22 we begin the third and final round, where only two of Job's friends speak. It brings us back to Eliphaz the Temanite, who by now is beginning to become very upset and angry. In fact, he loses his cool entirely and begins to pour out invective and accusation upon poor Job. Through this chapter he accuses Job of imaginary motives. Then he invents false charges against him; next, he assumes that Job holds rather insulting concepts, and he ends with some very inappropriate exhortations. First, the imagined motives:

> Then Eliphaz the Temanite answered:
> "Can a man be profitable to God?
>   Surely he who is wise is profitable to himself.
> Is it any pleasure [literally, profit] to the Almighty if you are righteous,
>   or is it gain to him if you make your ways blameless?"
> (22:1–3).

He is inferring that Job thinks he is defending himself to the glory and honor of God, that God's integrity is at stake. If Job confesses anything wrong, God will falter and fail thereby; God's image in the eyes of men depends on Job's ability to appear righteous. But Job never thought that at all. Throughout this account Job's view of God is that though he does not understand what God is doing, he sees him as a God of justice and righteousness. Though he is puzzled and uncertain and has no way of applying that view of God to his own situation at the moment, he never thinks of God as being anything other than a God of holiness. It is an entirely false charge.

Eliphaz goes on in verse 4:

> "Is it for your fear of him that he reproves you,
>   and enters into judgment with you?"

Here Eliphaz is suggesting that Job feels that God is unfairly punishing him, but once again, Job never said that. If he did he would be doing what Satan wanted him to do—he would be accusing and blaspheming God. It is true that Job asks God questions about his motives, but never once does he say, "You're at fault," and charge God with unrighteousness, as Eliphaz suggests.

Unsupported Charges

Perhaps this is one of the most helpful things we can learn from the Book of Job, because, in our testings, in our pressures, in our times of torment, Satan is also trying to get us to blame God and accuse him of being unfair and unjust. If we do that, we have fallen, we have gone over the brink and become guilty of an accusation against the God of righteousness. Job never does that. He comes very close, but he refuses to do that.

And so, upset and angry at Job's resistance to his charges, Eliphaz goes on to invent, out of the blue, unsupported charges against him:

> "Is not your wickedness great?
> There is no end to your iniquities.
> For you have exacted pledges of your brothers for nothing,
> and stripped the naked of their clothing.
> You have given no water to the weary to drink,
> and you have withheld bread from the hungry.
> The man with power possessed the land,
> and the favored man dwelt in it.
> You have sent widows away empty,
> and the arms of the fatherless were crushed.
> Therefore snares are round about you,
> and sudden terror overwhelms you;
> your light is darkened, so that you cannot see,
> and a flood of water covers you" (vv. 5–11).

Not one of these things was true; he simply begins to invent charges. This is the kind of Pharisaism that pours out invective against anyone who refuses to agree with its limited theology. In my wife's early Christian life she began listening to a radio broadcast that taught her truth from the Scriptures. The pastor of her church became very angry at her, and called her before him to try to straighten her out, using

personal demand instead of the Scriptures. When
she would not be persuaded because she was learning the truth from the Word of God, he did the
very thing Eliphaz did. He railed against her and
charged her with many things she had not done,
threatening to expose her to the church as a heretic.
She endured a great deal of mental torment and
suffering through that time. There is nothing worse
than this kind of unfounded, murderous, slanderous
attack.

Eliphaz goes on in verses 12 through 14 to make
rather insulting assumptions of the concepts that he
thinks Job holds:

> "Is not God high in the heavens?
>   See the highest stars, how lofty they are!
> Therefore you say, 'What does God know?
>   Can he judge through the deep darkness?
> Thick clouds enwrap him, so that he does not see,
>   and he walks on the vault of heaven.' "

This is a childish charge against Job. "The trouble
with you, Job, is you think God is such a limited
being he can't even see what you're doing. He's high
up in heaven and the clouds come in between and
shut you off. You think you're getting by with your
sin because God can't see through the clouds!" That
is ridiculous, for Job has already demonstrated he
has a consciousness of the mightiness, the greatness,
the majesty and the mystery of God far beyond that
of these friends.

Eliphaz goes on to charge him with only pretend-
ing to hate iniquity. In verses 15 through 20 he suggests that Job is saying he rejects the wicked and
their way of life when actually he holds to it. In
verses 17 and 18 Eliphaz mimics Job when he says
of the wicked:

"They said to God, 'Depart from us,'
  and 'What can the Almighty do to us?'
Yet he filled their houses with good things—
  but the counsel of the wicked is far from me."

Notice that Job said those very things in the last chapter, in verse 16. Eliphaz is mimicking him. "That is what you say, 'The counsel of the wicked is far from me,' but you don't mean it at all. You're just as wicked as the rest of them." So with this mockery and scorn he tries to break through Job's argument. Then he ends in beautifully phrased language, with inappropriate exhortations to Job to confess his sin and return to God, and God will pour out blessing upon him. All of this certainly is true, if Job could find the sin that they claim he is guilty of. But as he examines his life he knows there is nothing he has not dealt with.

That brings us then to chapters 23 and 24, and Job's expression of his deepest problem. At this point he does not even attempt to answer the arguments anymore. He simply cries out of a troubled heart, in the presence of these friends, expressing himself half to God and half to them. Eloquently he tells how he feels.

Why Is God Absent?

He asks two questions, one in chapter 23 and one in chapter 24. These are the great unanswered questions that men continually ask today, questions that lie at the root of much doubt and much unwillingness to accept the presence of God. In chapter 23 Job asks, "Why does God seem to be absent from human affairs?" He begins with expressing his own longing for God:

"Today also my complaint is bitter,
   his hand is heavy in spite of my groaning" (v.2).

He is having a bad day, physically, but he cries,

"Oh that I knew where I might find him,
   that I might come even to his seat!
I would lay my case before him
   and fill my mouth with arguments.
I would learn what he would answer me,
   and understand what he would say to me" (vv. 3–5).

As his pain increases his frustration grows because he cannot find any way to get into contact and argue the point with God and get some answers to his problem. And yet, in the midst of the darkness, there is an unshaken confidence in God. He says in verse 6,

"Would he contend with me in the greatness of his power?
   No; he would give heed to me.
There an upright man could reason with him,
   and I should be acquitted for ever by my judge."

As we have seen many times before, Job feels that if he would get a chance to lay the situation out before God as he sees it, God himself, in his basic justice, would admit that he was right. So he describes his search:

"Behold, I go forward, but he is not there;
   and backward, but I cannot perceive him;
on the left hand I seek him, but I cannot behold him;
   I turn to the right hand, but I cannot see him" (vv. 8, 9).

Have you ever felt that way—abandoned? You cannot find God, cannot find any answers in your search for relief from the mental torture that increases your doubt and troubles you. At this point Job again declares his own righteousness and his faith that God will see him through at last:

> "But he knows the way that I take;
>   when he has tried me, I shall come forth as gold" (v. 10).

That expresses a great deal of confidence that God is a God of justice. Job says, "I don't understand what I am going through. I feel I've been doing the right thing and still this torment goes on, but I know that God will explain it to me some day." That is as high as his faith can rise at the moment. Then he goes on to restate at some length his sense of righteousness.

Why Is God Silent?

In chapter 24 he raises the second question that many people have asked: "Why is God silent? Why doesn't he judge evil?"

> "Why are not times of judgment kept by the Almighty,
>   and why do those who know him never see his days?"

He goes on to describe vividly the conditions of life. Thieves and scoundrels flourish (vv. 2, 3); poor people suffer terribly, they are mistreated, they have to scratch for a living, and they are exposed to the elements (vv. 4–12).

> "They lie all night naked, without clothing,
>   and have no covering in the cold.
> They are wet with the rain of the mountains,
>   and cling to the rock for want of shelter" (vv. 7, 8).

He says that they are exploited by the rich; they work for nothing in their fields and fruit-groves. Finally they die or are wounded and cry out to God:

"From out of the city the dying groan,
   and the soul of the wounded cries for help;
   yet God pays no attention to their prayer" (v. 12).

Job goes on to describe how the criminals strike in the darkness, and God does nothing about it:

"The murderer rises in the dark,
   that he may kill the poor and needy;
   and in the night he is as a thief.
The eye of the adulterer also waits for the twilight . . ."
                                        (vv. 14, 15).

These adulterers slink around in the darkness, lurking there to do their evil deeds.

Then he faces the question, "Why does God delay justice?" Job says his friends argue that God invariably punishes the wicked (he sums up their argument in vv. 18–20), but he says the facts are quite different:

"They feed on the barren childless woman,
   and do no good to the widow.
Yet God prolongs the life of the mighty by his power;
   they rise up when they despair of life" (vv. 21, 22).

There are the two great questions that hang unanswered in life: Why is God absent when he is so needed? Why is he so silent when he should speak? It is only when we get into the New Testament that we get any direct revelation to help us with this. Both Paul and Peter tell us that these are but evidences of God's patience and longsuffering with men. Paul tells us in Romans, "His goodness is meant to lead us to repentance." So if we are getting by with things now, it is only because God is withholding his hand, that he might give us a chance to learn the truth about ourselves.

Peter says, "Don't accuse God of slowness in fulfilling his promises, as men count slowness, because God is not willing that any should perish but wants to give all a chance to come to repentance." That is why God lets these things go on sometimes. For if he started judging, he would have to include us, as well as everyone else. Job has not come to that answer yet. The questions remain unanswered at this point.

Now the final speaker comes in, Bildad the Shuhite, with a short address consisting of the same two arguments, worn out by now. First, God is all-powerful:

> "Dominion and fear are with God;
>   he makes peace in his high heaven" (v. 2).

There is no way of combating the greatness, the power, the wisdom and the insight of God. This is true, as is his second point:

> "How then can man be righteous before God?
>   How can he who is born of woman be clean?
> Behold, even the moon is not bright,
>   and the stars are not clean in his sight;
> how much less man, who is a maggot,
>   and the son of man, who is a worm!" (vv. 4–6).

Not Like a Worm

It is interesting to see that the Scriptures never treat man like a worm. God's view of man is that though he has turned his back upon light and plunged himself into darkness and is reaping the result of his own iniquity, God never treats him like a worm. He treats him like a deeply loved and valuable individual, to whom he is ready to commit himself in order to redeem him. This much is true: only when a man admits he cannot help himself, that he is indeed a wretched person, can he be helped. But God never treats him as a worm. Bildad here reflects a narrow theology that does not fit the facts.

In chapter 26 Job hangs up the phone. He says there is no use talking to them anymore. His answer to Bildad is rich in irony:

> "How you have helped him who has no power!
>   How you have saved the arm that has no strength!
> How you have counseled him who has no wisdom,
>   and plentifully declared sound knowledge!
> With whose help have you uttered words,
>   and whose spirit has come forth from you?" (vv. 2–4).

Sarcastic praise—suggesting that they have been of no help at all to him! Job does not see yet that God is using these friends in his life. Satan has sent them, but God is using them, and we will soon see the result in Job's life.

Once again he goes on to describe the majesty of God in a brilliant and moving passage, and he closes with this word, in verse 14:

> "Lo, these are but the outskirts of his ways;
>   and how small a whisper do we hear of him!
> But the thunder of his power who can understand?"

What he says is simply this: there is a mystery in God that no man can plumb. Even when we have understood something of the greatness of his wisdom and majesty in nature, when we have learned of his omnipresence, his omnipotence, and his omniscience, and we know that as part of our theology, it still does not explain all of his ways. God occupies a much bigger box than any of us can build.

In one of Robert Browning's poems he describes how a young man in the arrogance of his youth has worked out his philosophy so that God is no longer necessary. He comes to an old bishop and tells him he does not need God any longer. The old bishop says to him,

> Just when we're safest, there's a sunset-touch,
> A fancy from a flower-bell, someone's death,
> A chorus-ending from Euripides,—
> And that's enough for fifty hopes and fears . . .
> The grand Perhaps!

God cannot be excluded from his own universe. Job never makes that mistake, though he painfully seeks to answer the doubts that fling themselves at him in his darkness. As we shall see, his search will not go unrewarded.

Oswald Chambers says this of Job: "We must get hold of the great souls, the men who have been hard hit and have gone to the basis of things and whose experiences have been preserved for us by God, that we may know where we stand."

Heavenly Father, thank you for Job, and for the encouragement we receive from this book, to know that other men and women in the past have faced the same difficult questions that we have faced, and it has not shaken their faith. It has not overwhelmed them and knocked them off their feet and caused them to curse you and rebel against you. Help us to take heart in what trials we may be having, and to know that you will bring us through. Help us also to cry, with Job, "You know the way that we take; and when you have tried us, we shall come forth as gold." We pray in Christ's name, Amen.

7

The Wrong of Self-Defense

The world knows only two kinds of speakers: those who have something to say, and those who have to say something. Job's three friends are the latter kind. They have kept a dialogue going until it has finally ground to a halt. In chapter 26 we saw Job's final response to his friends, and now in chapters 27 through 31 he presents an extended soliloquy as his last defense. He opens with a firm statement of his resolve to stand fast to the end:

And Job again took up his discourse, and said,
"As God lives, who has taken away my right,
    and the Almighty, who has made my soul bitter;
as long as my breath is in me,
    and the spirit of God is in my nostrils;
my lips will not speak falsehood,
    and my tongue will not utter deceit.
Far be it from me to say that you are right;
    till I die I will not put away my integrity from me.

I hold fast my righteousness, and will not let it go;
  my heart does not reproach me for any of my days"
                                    27(vv. 1–6).

This is his sturdy answer to the persistent accusations of these friends. He says, "I am not going to say you are right." One cannot help but appreciate the spirit of this man who is determined to tell the truth, whatever it may cost him. Even at the price of peace he is not going to admit to something he did not do.

In some ways Job's answer recalls that famous scene in the great cathedral at Worms, Germany, when Martin Luther stood up for his faith. He was called before the assembled dignitaries, the nobles of empire, the princes of the Catholic Church, and even the Emperor himself, to be charged with heresy and put on trial for his life. Many have thrilled at his words as he closed his defense by saying, "Unless I am shown by the testimony of Scripture and by evident reasoning, unless I am overcome by means of the scriptural passages that I have cited, and unless my conscience is taken captive by the words of God, I am neither able nor willing to revoke anything, since to act against one's conscience is neither safe nor honest. Here I stand; God help me, I cannot do otherwise, amen!" Like Luther, Job is willing to stand firm on what he has said; he will not give in.

In verses 7 through 11, he warns these friends that if they are not careful they may be guilty of malicious accusation that will merit the very punishment from God they thought he deserved. In the law of Israel it was well known that if someone falsely charged another with a crime, the one who made the charge would ultimately himself be punished for that crime. In verse 7 he says,

> "Let my enemy be as the wicked,
> and let him that rises up against me be as the unrighteous."

The enemy he refers to here is these so-called "friends." In verses 13 through the end of the chapter Job repeats the arguments these friends have used. Job is saying, in effect, "Your own words will condemn you. If you have been falsely accusing me, you will be the ones who will be punished."
In verse 13 he says: *Ch 27*

> "This is the portion of a wicked man with God,
> and the heritage which oppressors receive from the Almighty: . . ."

Then he describes how their children will ultimately be killed by the sword; how they will heap up wealth and it will disappear in a day; how the wicked man goes to bed rich but wakes up poor; how terrors overtake him in a flood, and the east wind destroys him, and so on. He is warning these friends that if they continue with their accusations, such will be their fate.

A Search for Wisdom

Chapter 28 is one of the most beautiful chapters of the book. It is Job's meditation on his endless search for an explanation of what he is going through. He describes it as a search for wisdom. The first 11 verses are a vivid description of the way men search in the earth for hidden treasure, for gold and precious stones. Remember, Job is the oldest book in the Bible; it comes from the very dawn of civilization. Yet here we have a description of mining practices that sounds as though it was taken out of contemporary life:

"Surely there is a mine for silver,
   and a place for gold which they refine.
Iron is taken out of the earth,
   and copper is smelted from the ore" (vv. 1, 2).

Then he describes how the miners work:

"Men put an end to darkness,
   and search out to the farthest bound
   the ore in gloom and deep darkness.
      [Putting an end to darkness refers to the little lamps
      that miners use as they go into the dark shafts of the
      earth.]
They open shafts in a valley away from where men live;
   they are forgotten by travelers,
   they hang afar from men, they swing to and fro"
                                              (vv. 3, 4).

He is referring to scaffolding that is erected on the side of a mountain so that miners can get up into the mines and find the treasures that are there.

In verses 7 and 8 Job says there is nothing in nature like a man's desperate search for gold:

"That path no bird of prey knows,
   and the falcon's eye has not seen it.
The proud beasts have not trodden it;
   the lion has not passed over it."

Animals pay no attention to gold and jewels; it is only men who seek after these things. And they will go to any limits to find them. He goes on:

"Man puts his hand to the flinty rock,
  and overturns mountains by the roots.
He cuts out channels in the rocks,
  and his eye sees every precious thing.
He binds up the streams so that they do not trickle,
  and the thing that is hid he brings forth to light"
(vv. 9–11).

Miners often must dam up water that seeps into their mines in order to work them. Job shows how man gives up almost anything and goes to any lengths to find gold. Then he comes to his point:

"But where shall wisdom be found?
  And where is the place of understanding?
Man does not know the way to it,
  and it is not found in the land of the living.
The deep says, 'It is not in me,'
  and the sea says, 'It is not with me'" (vv. 12–14).

Here we see the reason for his analogy of the search for gold and silver. He says men will go to any lengths to find that treasure, and so also do they look for the answers to the riddles of life. They can find the gold by their efforts, but they cannot find wisdom. He is emphasizing the elusiveness of wisdom.

What is this wisdom Job is talking about? Once my wife and I were invited to dinner by a naval officer. We noticed as he led us into the officer's club that he walked with a cane. Inquiring of some other friends, we learned that he was suffering from melanoma, a cancer that was threatening his life. The friend said also that this man had lost two sons at the age of 19 from cancer, and just that week he had received word that his 14-year-old son also had cancer. Our hearts went out to him, but his spirit was strong and triumphant. He was gracious to all, saying no word of this himself, and he appeared to be a man utterly free from care. But our hearts cried out, "Why? Why do these kinds of things happen?" Life presents such riddles to us as it did also to Job. Wisdom is the answer to that question, "Why?"

Wisdom is the knowledge of the nature of things, the understanding of the reasons behind what happens. Someone has described wisdom as the right use of knowledge, and as far as it goes that is a good description. We do many things with knowledge but we do not always do the right things with it. That is why knowledge of nuclear physics can end up with atom bombs and other malicious instruments of warfare and widespread destruction. Man lacks the wisdom to use his knowledge in right ways. Though he can learn *how* things happen, he does not know *why*.

I read recently that a distinguished astro-physicist in Sweden has stated that the book of Genesis ought to start this way: "In the beginning there was an original cloud, magnetized, and perhaps a light-year [6 trillion miles] in diameter." That sounds very impressive. But there are two questions of supreme importance that the learned professor needs to answer: first, of what was the original cloud made, and second, who put it there? Only God knows, for wisdom belongs to him. Someone has said, "Any man can tell how many seeds there are in an apple, but only God knows how many apples there are in a seed."

In verses 15 to 19 Job declares that wisdom cannot be bought—it cannot be found and it cannot be bought.

"It cannot be gotten for gold,
    and silver cannot be weighted as its price.
It cannot be valued in the gold of Ophir,
    in precious onyx or sapphire.
Gold and glass cannot equal it,
    nor can it be exchanged for jewels of fine gold.
No mention shall be made of coral or of crystal;
    the price of wisdom is above pearls.
The topaz of Ethiopia cannot compare with it,
    nor can it be valued in pure gold."

If wisdom could be bought, the rich would be the happiest people on earth. But oftentimes they are the most miserable of people, having lost even the simplest enjoyments of life.

The Fear of the Lord

Well, where does wisdom come from? How do you find these elusive answers? Job tells us:

"God understands the way to it,
    and he knows its place.
For he looks to the ends of the earth,
    and sees everything under the heavens.
        [God knows where it is, and God knows what it is.]
When he gave to the wind its weight,
    and meted out the waters by measure;
when he made a decree for the rain,
    and a way for the lightning of the thunder;
then he saw it and declared it;
    he established it, and searched it out" (vv. 23–27).

There is a wonderful scientific accuracy running through the analogies that Job uses in this passage. For many centuries men did not know that wind had weight, but Job knew it. Also, "God measures out the waters, and makes a decree for rain; he makes a special way for the lightning." These have counterparts in the scientific discoveries of our day, but Job seemed to understand these things. He said, in effect, that God made wisdom when he created the universe. He understood what he was doing and he understood how it would work and all the problems that would be involved. Thus only God knows wisdom. But in verse 28 Job tells us the only way to find it:

"And he said to man,
'Behold, the fear of the Lord, that is wisdom;
    and to depart from evil is understanding.' "

28:28

"The fear of the Lord, that is wisdom." That is, when a person stands before God in respectful, loving trust, understanding that he is a God who knows what he is doing, that is the beginning of wisdom. The Book of Proverbs also declares this. You will never be able to answer the riddles of your life until you come to that place. If you want to discover wisdom, then begin to obey and do what God says. Many can give testimony to the fact that this is what began to unravel for them the riddles of life. This is also what Job came to understand.

In the next three chapters he reviews for us all that has happened to him. In chapter 29 he is looking back at the good old days. First he tells us of his blessings:

And Job again took up his discourse, and said,
"Oh, that I were as in the months of old,
    as in the days when God watched over me;
when his lamp shone upon my head,
    and by his light I walked through darkness;

as I was in my autumn days,
> when the friendship of God was upon my tent;
when the Almighty was yet with me,
> when my children were about me;
when my steps were washed with milk,
> and the rock poured out for me streams of oil!"

(vv. 1–6).

This is beautiful poetry, describing those halcyon days when God's smile was upon him, and all the blessing of life was his.

Then he describes the honor that he experienced:

"When I went out to the gate of the city,
> when I prepared my seat in the square,
the young men saw me and withdrew,
> and the aged rose and stood;
the princes refrained from talking,
> and laid their hand on their mouth;
the voice of the nobles was hushed.
> and their tongue cleaved to the roof of their mouth"

(vv. 7–10).

Then he speaks of the good deeds he delighted in doing:

". . . I delivered the poor who cried,
and the fatherless who had none to help him" (v. 12).

". . . I caused the widow's heart to sing for joy" (v. 13).

"I was eyes to the blind,
> and feet to the lame" (v. 15).

"I was a father to the poor . . ." (v. 16).

"I broke the fangs of the unrighteous,
> and made him drop his prey from his teeth" (v. 17).

In verses 18 through 20 he tells us what his hopes were:

29; 18-26

"Then I thought, 'I shall die in my nest,
   and I shall multiply my days as the sand,
my roots spread out to the waters,
   with the dew all night on my branches,
my glory fresh with me,
   and my bow ever new in my hand.'"

Job had felt that this ought to go on to the end—
the man who serves God will be taken care of by
God and will never be put to any trouble or problem.
Many Christians view life in the same way. "If I
obey God and serve God and do what I know to
be right, God will prosper me, bless me and take
care of me, and I will never be exposed to any evil
or pressure." But Job's experience has blown that
philosophy to bits, though he does not understand
it.

He concludes the section by describing his influence, and how men listened to him. They waited
for him as for the rain, and he smiled on them. In
fact, he says:

"I chose their way, and sat as chief,
   and I dwelt like a king among his troops,
   like one who comforts mourners" (v. 25).

"How I wish the good old days would return," Job
is saying.

The Painful Present

Now in chapter 30 we get the other side, the painful present. He begins in the first 15 verses by describing how men mock him:

"But now they make sport of me,
   men who are younger than I,

    whose fathers I would have disdained
       to set with the dogs of my flock" (v. 1).

Job goes on to describe the character of these men,
how they are evil, narrow, rigid, unpleasant people.
And yet:

    "And now I have become their song,
       I am a byword to them.
    They abhor me, they keep aloof from me;
       they do not hesitate to spit at the sight of me"
                                   (vv. 9, 10).

    In verses 11 to 15 he describes their insults and
their attacks, and then in verses 16 to 19, the anguish
of his physical pain:

    "And now my soul is poured out within me;
       days of affliction have taken hold of me.
    The night racks my bones,
       and the pain that gnaws me takes no rest.
    With violence it seizes my garment;
       it binds me about like the collar of my tunic.
    God has cast me into the mire.
       and I have become like dust and ashes."

    Then the worst thing of all for him to bear, the
silence of God, is described in verses 20 through
26:

    "I cry to thee and thou dost not answer me;
       I stand, and thou dost not heed me."

    Job goes on to describe how he feels persecuted
by God. He cries out to him "as one who in a heap
of ruins stretches out his hand," but God does not

listen. This is the problem many have in times of pressure and pain—unanswered prayer, unexplained violence, and unfulfilled hopes. That, Job says, is what hurts the most. So he concludes the chapter with a description of the misery of living:

> "My heart is in turmoil, and is never still;
>   days of affliction come to meet me.
> I go about blackened, but not by the sun;
>   I stand up in the assembly, and cry for help.
> I am a brother of jackals,
>   and a companion of ostriches.
> My skin turns black and falls from me,
>   and my bones burn with heat.
> My lyre is turned to mourning,
>   and my pipe to the voice of those who weep"
>   (vv. 27–31).

Chapter 31 describes Job's last search for a reason for all this. He is going back now and trying to find an answer; he is still searching for wisdom. His theology has not yet stretched beyond the explanation that some sin may be causing this, so he reviews his life from that point of view.

First, he says, there have been no sexual misdeeds in his life:

> "I have made a covenant with my eyes;
>   how then could I look upon a virgin?" (v. 1).

Even this early in the history of the world Job has learned that to keep clean before God he has to be careful about what he sees. He makes a covenant with his eyes. To properly handle his sexual drives he must watch his thought life. If he does not, he realizes, "Calamity will befall the unrighteous, and disaster the workers of iniquity" (v. 3). He invites people to investigate and see if he is not truthful in this. If anyone has found him to be a liar, he says:

> "then let me sow, and another eat;
> and let what grows for me be rooted out" (v. 8).

He has kept clean from the sin of fornication, and he says in verses 9 through 12, there has been no adultery either:

> "If my heart has been enticed to a woman,
> and I have lain in wait at my neighbor's door,
> then let my wife grind for another,
> and let others bow down upon her" (vv. 9, 10).

He is willing to bear this punishment because he understands that to commit adultery

> ". . . would be a heinous crime;
> that would be an iniquity to be punished by the judges; for
> that would be a fire which consumes unto Abaddon [destruction],
> and it would burn to the root of all my increase"
> (vv. 11, 12).

Then, next, he points out there has been no injustice in his deeds. He has been just with his servants; he has been just toward the poor and the defenseless. There has been no trust in wealth (vv. 24, 25) and no secret idolatry (vv. 26, 28). He has not gloated over the misfortune of others (vv. 29, 30); he has not been stingy with his wealth (vv. 31, 32). There is no hypocrisy in his affairs, he has not been keeping things secret (vv. 33, 37).

Finally, he has not abused the land, he has not caused any pollution of the environment. How relevant this book of Job is!

"If my land has cried out against me,
   and its furrows have wept together;
if I have eaten its yield without payment,
   and caused the death of its owners;
let thorns grow instead of wheat,
   and foul weeds instead of barley" (vv. 38–40).

With this stout disclaimer the words of Job are ended; he has nothing more to say. Baffled, questioning, tormented, yet unwilling to forsake God, he falls silent.

At this point there comes a noticeable break in the book. Another voice is heard, a young man's voice, which will help Job (and us) find the answers he seeks. For by now, we too sit where Job sits. Job's questions become our questions. What can we say about the trials, the pressures and the riddles of our own lives? Job has learned by now that his theology is too small for his God. God is greater than any study man can make of him, yet he is never inconsistent with himself. He is not capricious, nor acting out of malice. He is a loving God, but his love will be expressed in forms that we do not always understand, and we must face that fact. Up to this point Job has had faith in the rule of God, but now, at last, he has begun tremblingly to exercise faith in the God who rules. That is a transfer that many of us need to learn.

Depths of Sin

The second thing we can see at this point is that Job's view of himself is woefully inadequate. He has been defending himself, just as we do when trouble strikes. We all tend to think, *I haven't done anything wrong. I've been perfectly well-behaved. Why should I be subjected to this kind of torment?* As we watch Job, we realize that we too have little understanding of the depths of sin's attack upon us, and the depravity of our hearts. Jeremiah says, "The heart is deceitful above all things and desperately wicked. Who can know it?" One thing God teaches us by these pressures and problems is to understand that there are depths of sin within us of which we are not yet aware. We need to hear Paul's words in chapter 4 of 1 Corinthians, "But with me it is a very small thing that I should be judged by you or by any human court. I do not even judge myself. I am not aware of anything against myself [i.e., that he had not dealt with], but I am not thereby acquitted." Paul understands that God knows more about him than he knows about himself.

The third thing we learn is that God's silence is explained by Job's self-vindication. Why does God not help this man? The answer is that he has not yet come to the place where he is willing to listen. As long as a man is defending himself, God will not defend him. This is a theme that runs all through the Bible from beginning to end. As long as Job thinks he has some righteous ground on which to stand, God remains silent. This is true with us as well. Jesus begins the Sermon on the Mount by saying, "Blessed is the man who is poor in spirit," i.e., who is bankrupt in himself, who has come to the end of himself. When we stop defending and justifying ourselves, God will step in to take up our cause. That is what we find in the Book of Job; God will soon begin to speak on Job's behalf for Job has now been reduced to silence.

In the little book of 1 John we read, ". . . if any one does sin, we have an advocate with the Father,

Jesus Christ the righteous." Jesus is our lawyer, our defense counselor. But as long as we keep trying to justify and explain everything on the basis of our goodness, he has nothing to say. When we quit, then he rises up to take our case before God the Father. This is probably the greatest lesson of the Book of Job, but surely the one that is hardest for us to learn.

Our Father, this marvelous book has taken us through deep waters indeed, and has deepened our understanding and our knowledge of you. We pray that, like Job, we will realize that there is no solution to the riddles and mysteries of life apart from a trust in your wisdom and your grace, and an obedience to your Word. Help us then to lay aside all our flaunting schemes for self-improvement and defense of ourselves, and to stand naked before you, Lord, trusting your loving grace to give us all we need. We ask in Jesus' name, Amen.

8

Youth Answers Age

In chapter 32 we come to a rather sudden and unexpected shift in the development of the Book of Job. A new voice is heard, a new name appears, without much introduction. The program notes of this cosmic drama give us some information in the opening verses of the chapter:

So these three men ceased to answer Job, because he was righteous in his own eyes. Then Elihu the son of Barachel the Buzite, of the family of Ram, became angry. He was angry at Job because he justified himself rather than God; he was angry also at Job's three friends because they had found no answer, although they had declared Job to be in the wrong. Now Elihu had waited to speak to Job because they were older than he. And when Elihu saw that there was no answer in the mouth of these three men, he became angry.

One is tempted to ask about this young man, Elihu, "Who is this fellow? Where did he come from, and

123

why does he speak at this moment?" We learn from this interjection that there were others who were listening to the dialogue between Job and his three friends. Among them is Elihu, a name which means, "My God is he." He is also identified as the son of Barachel (which means "God blesses"), the Buzite. In the opening of the book we learned that Job lived in the land of Uz, but there was another land nearby called Buz (these lands were named for two brothers who lived in the days following Noah and the flood), and Elihu came from the land of Buz; we know nothing more about him.

In chapter 32 we have the introduction to his message, which opens with a word of courteous explanation for his silence:

> And Elihu the son of Barachel the Buzite answered:
> "I am young in years,
>   and you are aged;
> therefore I was timid and afraid
>   to declare my opinion to you.
> I said, 'Let days speak,
>   and many years teach wisdom.'
> But it is the spirit in a man,
>   and breath of the Almighty, that makes him understand.
> It is not the old that are wise,
>   nor the aged that understand what is right.
> Therefore I say, 'Listen to me;
>   let me also declare my opinion' " (vv. 6–10).

Commentators seem to differ widely in what to make of Elihu. Some regard him as a rather brash young man, characterized by the cocksure arrogance of youth, who seeks to show the older men where they are wrong. Others see him as merely repeating the same arguments of the three friends, without adding much. Still other commentators view this discourse as a kind of meaningless interruption in the dialogue, of which God takes no notice at all.

A Major Role

But there are also commentators (with whom I agree), who see Elihu as playing a very important part in this book. Let us note certain things about this young man. First, in the rebuke God gives to the three friends of Job at the end of the book, it is noteworthy that Elihu is not included. He is not rebuked for what he says, nor does he have to ask Job to pray for him, as the three friends are told to do. The second thing is that he is given an obvious, prominent part in this drama. His message occupies the next five chapters and is one of the major discourses of this book. Third, he always speaks with courtesy and sensitivity to Job, despite the strong feelings which he confesses. The other friends were caustic and sarcastic in their approach to Job but this young man is courteous when he addresses him. He recognizes the depth of Job's suffering, and always speaks with understanding, though often in rebuke.

Fourth, and probably most important, Elihu claims to speak not from experience as the other men did, but from revelation. That is what we understand from verse 8, where Elihu says, "It is the spirit in a man, the breath of the Almighty, that makes him understand." This is in line with what we have seen previously in Job, that knowledge is something gained over the years, but understanding and wisdom can come only from God. Furthermore, he can give it to the young as well as the old. The accumulation of years of experience is not what makes people wise; it is what God has taught them through the years. When we speak from the wisdom of God we can truly be wise, regardless of our calendar age.

Sometimes we who have been young a long time tend to think it is the years that have made us wise! I once heard of a schoolteacher who applied for a job but was passed over in preference to another younger teacher who only had three years of experience. The first teacher protested to the principal, "I've had 25 years' experience. Why was I passed over in favor of this younger one?" The principal said, "I'm sorry to disagree with you. You haven't had 25 years' experience. You've had one year's experience 25 times!" So Elihu is right. It is not necessarily the old who are wise, nor the aged who understand; it is the spirit of the Almighty who teaches us wisdom.

God's Answer

Elihu comes into the book as the answer to Job's cry for an explanation. God has been silent, it seems, and though Job is suffering and cries out for help, no answer is given. But in God's wonderful way he replies in a manner which Job did not expect. This young man has been listening all along. Suddenly he speaks up and appears as a witness to the mediator for whom Job has been crying out all through the book. Elihu is a kind of John the Baptist of the Old Testament. He gives witness to the Mediator who is God himself. John said that he was a voice crying in the wilderness, pointing to One who would make a ransom between man and God. So Elihu appears as the one who gives witness to what Job is calling for, an umpire who can lay his hand upon both man and God. He begins where the friends began, but he ends with words very similar to the voice of God when at last God appears on the scene.

In this introduction, from verse 11 on, he speaks of his patience which is now nearly exhausted. He first addresses the three friends:

> "Behold, I waited for your words,
>   I listened for your wise sayings,
>   while you searched out what to say.
> I gave you my attention
>   and, behold, there was none that confuted Job,
>   or that answered his words, among you.
> Beware lest you say, 'We have found wisdom;
>   God may vanquish him, not man.'
> He has not directed his words against me,
>   and I will answer him with your speeches" (vv. 11–14).

Then, further describing the friends, he says,

> "They are discomfited, they answer no more;
>   they have not a word to say.
> And shall I wait, because they do not speak,
>   because they stand there, and answer no more?"
>   (vv. 15, 16).

So, with that forthright word of explanation, he begins to speak. He declares he has to say something for he feels much pressure within:

> "I also will give my answer;
>   I also will declare my opinion.
> For I am full of words,
>   the spirit within me constrains me.
> Behold, my heart is like wine that has no vent;
>   like new wineskins, it is ready to burst" (vv. 17–19).

Have you ever felt that way, listening to an argument? It's as if you had to say something because you saw the discussion was going astray. It was illogical, and you could hardly restrain from speaking. Elihu says, "I must speak, that I may find relief." Then he reassures Job and the friends:

"I will not show partiality to any person
or use flattery toward any man.
For I do not know how to flatter,
else would my Maker soon put an end to me"
(vv. 21, 22).

Chapter 33 contains Elihu's address to Job. It opens with an invitation to dialogue:

"But now, hear my speech, O Job,
and listen to all my words.
Behold, I open my mouth;
the tongue in my mouth speaks.
My words declare the uprightness of my heart,
and what my lips know they speak sincerely" (vv. 1–3).

Here is his promise to give honest words. He is not going to flatter, and he is not going to speak out of experience; he is going to speak from what he has been taught. His words will be honest and without partiality. And further, he goes on to say, they will come from a humble heart:

"The spirit of God has made me,
and the breath of the Almighty gives me life.
Answer me, if you can;
set your words in order before me; take your stand.
Behold, I am toward God as you are;
I too was formed from a piece of clay.
Behold, no fear of me need terrify you;
my pressure will not be heavy upon you" (vv. 4–7).

How different from the way the friends spoke to Job! This young man says, "I'm only a man, like you. What I may say to help has come from what God has taught me. But I'm like you are, and I'm not going to accuse you or come on heavy against you. I'm speaking merely as God has taught me, as the Spirit of God has given me life."

Then, beginning with verse 8, he begins to analyze Job's view of God.

God Is Greater Than Man

Job's first wrong view of God, according to Elihu, is that he sees God as capricious, acting out of his feelings (like people do), and according to his mood:

> "Surely, you have spoken in my hearing,
>   and I have heard the sound of your words.
> You say, 'I am clean, without transgression;
>   I am pure, and there is no iniquity in me.
> Behold, he [God] finds occasions against me,
>   he counts me as his enemy;
> he puts my feet in the stocks,
>   and watches all my paths'" (vv. 8–11).

Here he summarizes all the things Job has been saying—that God mistreats him without a reason; that he is doing these things without justification, in a capricious way. Elihu's answer is in one short word:

> "Behold, in this you are not right, I will answer you"
>
> (v. 12).

And here is his answer:

33; 12

> "God is greater than man."

That is what we must always remember about God. He is beyond us. His range of understanding is infinitely greater than ours. Man is too ignorant, too limited, too easily deceived (his history proves it), to ever lay a charge of capriciousness against God. God always acts in accordance with his nature of love. Behind every act of God is a loving heart. And when we do not think so, it is we who are deceived, it is we who are misjudging. We do not see what he is after.

This is the continual argument of the Bible. In the ninth chapter of Romans Paul says; "Who are you, O man, that replies against God?" "Why, you're nothing but a creature with very limited experience and understanding. You don't even know all the facts involved. How then can you raise a challenge against the Creator who sees so much more?" God is greater than man. So with that brief word Elihu puts this question to rest.

Then he moves to the second problem Job had with God. It was the matter of the silence of God:

> "Why do you contend against him,
>   saying, 'He will answer none of my words'?
> For God speaks in one way,
>   and in two, though man does not perceive it"
>
>   (vv. 13, 14).

Once again, one of the major problems we struggle with is the silence of God—unanswered prayer, we call it. We complain that our prayers are not answered because we prayed ten days ago and the answer has not come yet. God is responsible to come back with an immediate answer, we think. But Elihu helps us with this problem. He says God does speak, but sometimes in ways we do not recognize. There are two ways Elihu suggests. First, God speaks in dreams:

"In a dream, in a vision of the night,
　when deep sleep falls upon men,
　while they slumber on their beds.
then he opens the ears of men,
　and terrifies them with warnings,
that he may turn man aside from his deed,
　and cut off pride from man;
he keeps back his soul from the Pit,
his life from perishing by the sword" (vv. 15–18).

Notice how clearly he states that God's objective with man is to stop him from destroying himself. It is man who is bent upon destruction and the distress and pain he feels are God's warnings designed to keep him from hurting himself and others—"to keep back his soul from the Pit, his life from perishing by the sword." One of the ways God does that is to speak in dreams. Perhaps you say, "Surely you're not going to tell us we have to start analyzing our dreams." It is true that not all dreams come from God speaking to us. (Some of them come from eating pizza too late at night!) But psychologists tell us, as one voice, that dreams are a way by which suppressed reality comes into our consciousness, whether we like it or not.

We all tend to deceive ourselves. Things that we do not like to face we put away, we shove them down into the subconscious, and so they appear in our dreams. Oftentimes they take the form of warnings, in which we see ourselves doing things we are ashamed of or horrified by. These are warnings that the tendency, the possibility of doing wrong, is deep

within us. Watch what you are thinking. It is beginning to show up in your dreams! Although I am not
trying to build a case for interpreting dreams, the
Scriptures are full of instances where God does speak
to men in dreams. Daniel and Ezekiel and others
of the prophets understood much from God by
means of dreams. God does speak in dreams to us
sometimes, not to predict the future, but to show
us what we are trying to hide from ourselves in the
present.

God Is Shouting

Then the second thing Elihu says is that God also
speaks through pain:

> "Man is also chastened with pain upon his bed,
>   and with continual strife in his bones,
> so that his life loathes bread,
>   and his appetite dainty food.
> His flesh is so wasted away that it cannot be seen;
>   and his bones which were not seen stick out.
> His soul draws near the Pit,
>   and his life to those who bring death" (vv. 19–22).

Here Eilhu's argument seems deliberately to describe all that Job has gone through. The young man
is saying, "God is speaking to you, Job. You think
he is not saying anything? He is. Your very sufferings
are speaking to you. But not as the friends were
arguing, to punish you for something you did that
you're trying to hide, because that isn't true. God
is helping you to understand something that you
don't yet understand, and pain is what makes it possible."

Many of us have had the experience of feeling a

threat to our life from some illness. It tends to do marvelous things to our view of life; our value system changes almost instantly. We begin to see certain things as of far more importance than we had ever thought before. C. S. Lewis says this about pain:

> We can rest contentedly in our sins and in our stupidities, and everyone who has watched gluttons shoveling down the most exquisite foods as if they did not know what they were eating, will admit that we can ignore even pleasure. But pain insists upon being attended to. God whispers to us in our pleasures, speaks in our consciences, but shouts in our pains. It is his megaphone to rouse a deaf world.*

Have you ever had God shout at you through pain? A man said to me the other day, "I lived for a long time thinking that business was the most important thing in life, but then I had a heart attack and, believe me, God got my attention." Why do we have to wait until after our second heart attack before God gets our attention? God in love brings these things upon us that he might speak to us, that we will hear what he has to say.

Interpreted by a Mediator

Elihu goes on to bring out a second point about pain:

> "If there be for him an angel,
>   a mediator, one of the thousand,
>   to declare to man what is right for him;
> and he is gracious to him, and says,
>   'Deliver him from going down into the Pit,
>   I have found a ransom:

---

* C. S. Lewis, *The Problem of Pain* (New York: Macmillan, 1943), p. 93.

let his flesh become fresh with youth;
    let him return to the days of his youthful vigor' "
                                              33   (vv. 23–25).

Those last words seem to describe the experience
that we would call today "being born again," a return
to the freshness and vitality of youth. And what
brings it about? Well, as Elihu says, it is the presence
in the midst of our pains of a mediator, one of the
thousand, who declares to man what is right and
provides a ransom for him.

What an amazing foreview this is of the gospel
of the grace of God! Remember Paul argues this in
Romans 5. He says, "We rejoice in our sufferings."
Why? Because in our sufferings we're being taught
by God that he is working out purposes we do not
understand but which are for our good. And through
the love of God shed abroad in our hearts we can
realize that God's love is training us, steadying us
and teaching us through the time of stress. That is
why suffering, when it is interpreted by the mediator
whom God provides, is a blessing to us. But suffering
without that mediation produces bitterness, resentment, anger, frustration, and rebellion against God's
will. Therefore, there must be a mediator, Elihu says.

This is probably a reference to the slow and certain
light that has been growing in Job's heart all through
this time of suffering. He is beginning to understand
something about life that he never knew before. In
chapter 9 he cried out, "There is no umpire between
us that may lay his hand upon us both, man and
God." But in chapter 16 he said, "Even now, behold
my witness is in heaven, and he who vouches for
me is on high." He sees God is going to be the mediator. In chapter 19 he comes out clearly and cries,

"I know that my redeemer lives, and on the earth shall stand. And though worms destroy my body, yet in my flesh shall I see God face to face."

In chapter 23 he declared, "He knows the way that I take. When he has tried me, I shall come forth as gold."

Now here Elihu reminds him of that ministry of the mediator and tells him that if he allows the mediator's work to guide him through this time, he will be restored, his flesh will come fresh with youth, and he will return to the days of his youthful vigor. And then he gives him the means of doing this:

"Then man prays to God, and he accepts him,
     he comes into his presence with joy,
He recounts to men his salvation,
     and he sings before men, and says,
'I sinned, and perverted what was right,
     and it was not requited to me.
     [God did not punish me for what I did.]
He has redeemed my soul from going down into the Pit,
     and my life shall see the light'" (vv. 26–28).

Pain did that, and so Elihu exhorts Job:

"Behold, God does all these things,
     twice, three times, with a man" (v. 29).

How patient God is! How long he waits and allows us to meditate on and struggle with these things. He will sometimes bring us back to them again and again till we understand. So Elihu cries:

"Give heed, O Job, listen to me;
     be silent, and I will speak.
If you have anything to say, answer me;
     speak, for I desire to justify you.

If not, listen to me;
    be silent, and I will teach you wisdom" (vv. 31–33).

The silence of Job at this point seems to indicate that at last he is ready to listen. God is able to teach him what the heart and the meaning of all this suffering has been in his life. When Elihu finishes, God himself begins to speak, as we shall see.

Heavenly Father, we thank you for your loving care of us. We thank you for the Lord Jesus who came as the great Mediator, who found a ransom for us in his own life's blood poured out on our behalf; who has found a way to set aside the daily contamination of our sins and helps us to face every day fresh and vital, forgiven, alive, without guilt, without a sense of rejection, having found an adequate power by which to live, and do the things we ought to do. Lord, we thank you for the peace, the joy, the hope and the love that he has brought into our lives. In Jesus' name, Amen.

9

Your God Is Too Small

The young man, Elihu, has given a general examination of Job's problem, but in chapter 34 he takes up Job's view of God in some detail. He opens with an invitation to all who are listening to join in the judgment:

Then Elihu said,
"Hear my words, you wise men,
  and give ear to me, you who know;
For the ear tests words
  as the palate tastes food.
  [He is actually quoting the words of Job here.]
Let us choose what is right;
  let us determine among ourselves what is good"
                              34   (vv. 1–4).

This is one of several scriptural invitations to reason with God, to let our minds follow along the paths that God's great mind has already been. Isaiah said, "Come now, let us reason together, says the Lord:

Though your sins are like scarlet, they shall be as white as snow; though they are red like crimson, they shall become like wool." In 1 Corinthians the apostle Paul says, "I speak as to sensible men; judge for yourselves what I say."

Here is an invitation to join in judging the truth of what Elihu is about to say about God. He begins by examining once again Job's view of God:

> "For Job has said, 'I am innocent,
>   and God has taken away my right;
> in spite of my right I am counted a liar;
>   my wound is incurable, though I am without transgression' " (vv. 5, 6).

Job's problem is that he sees God as both unjust and unfair, and unwilling to explain what is going on. So Eilhu says:

> "What man is like Job,
>   who drinks up scoffing like water,
> who goes in company with evildoers
>   and walks with wicked men?
> For he has said, 'It profits a man nothing
>   that he should take delight in God' " (vv. 7–9).

What a strange statement from a man who began with the great cry, "The Lord gave, and the Lord has taken away. Blessed be the name of the Lord." Now (as Elihu says), he has become like the ungodly. He has the same attitude they have. He says, "What advantage is it to me to behave myself? I might just as well have sinned." That is the argument that will be examined in detail in this passage.

How many of us have said the same thing? At the beginning of this book Satan declared he was

going to bring Job to a place where he would curse
God to his face. To do so he must first make Job
distrust God and feel that God has treated him unfairly, and then, Satan hopes, there will come a time
when he will actually curse God, shake his fist in
God's face, and turn his back on him. Now Job has
come close to this, but he has not done it yet and
he does not do it. God intervenes by the wise words
of this Spirit-filled young man to keep Job from that
final step.

Always True to His Character

In verses 10 through 30, Elihu takes up the truth
about God. First, he says God cannot be unjust:

"Therefore, hear me, you men of understanding,
  far be it from God that he should do wickedness,
  and from the Almighty that he should do wrong.
For according to the work of a man he will requite him,
  and according to his ways he will make it befall him.
Of a truth, God will not do wickedly.
  and the Almighty will not pervert justice" (vv. 10–12).

No matter how long is may take, God will judge
the wicked and bless the righteous. He may not do
it right away, but he will do it. For, Elihu declares,
God cannot deny himself, he cannot be unjust. When
we say that God treats us unfairly or does something
wrong, we are really saying that God is denying his
own nature and character.

Earlier in the book Job's friends had argued this
point: God is so mighty that no matter what he says,
man has to accept it. But Elihu is not saying this.
He certainly agrees that God is mighty, yet all he
does is in accordance with his nature. In James God

is called "the Father of lights with whom is no varia-
tion or shadow due to change." There is no changea-
bility in God; he is always true to his character of
love, and we are invited to believe that, no matter
what it may look like to us at the moment. Such
faith will rescue us from that kind of temptation
Job is confronted with now.

Elihu's next point is that God is beyond accounta-
bility to man:

> "Who gave him charge over the earth
>   and who laid on him the whole world?
> If he should take back his spirit to himself,
>   and gather to himself his breath,
> all flesh would perish together,
>   and man would return to dust" (vv. 13–15).

Godless men are forever saying to God, in effect,
"Leave me alone. I don't need you. I don't want
you in my life." Now what if God actually did that?
What if he removed himself totally from them? They
would collapse instantly. It is God who gives them
the very breath they breathe. The man or woman
who speaks out against the Creator and challenges
God is doing so by the very power God himself supplies. Elihu asks, "Who gave him charge over the
earth?" Well, no man did. God is sovereign. He is
the originator of all things. He is therefore not ac-
countable to us.

Elihu's third point is that men get their sense of
justice from God; it is he who teaches us justice:

> "If you have understanding, hear this;
>   listen to what I say.
> Shall one who hates justice govern?
>   Will you condemn him who is righteous and mighty,

who says to a king, 'Worthless one,'
  and to nobles, 'Wicked man';
who shows no partiality to princes,
  nor regards the rich no more than the poor, for they are
  all the work of his hands?
In a moment they die;
  at midnight the people are shaken and pass away, and
  the mighty are taken away by no human hand"

3 4 (vv. 16–20).

We who prate so loudly about justice, and demand that God treat us with justice, are the very ones who offer flattery to rulers or show partiality to people who are in authority. God does not do that. Elihu argues here that God governs without partiality, and how can one do that without justice? Can man be more just than God? It is from God that human ideas of justice derive.

No Investigating Committee

Elihu's fourth point is that God does not need to make investigation before he judges. These days if a man wants to inquire into the justice of something, the first thing he must do is to appoint an investigating committee. Then he has to get funds for the committee, set up their offices and hire the secretaries, and then, after a couple of years' labor, they finally come up with a conclusion. But by that time someone has found that the committee was bribed or corrupted in some way, so another committee must be appointed to investigate the investigating committee. That is man's way. But Elihu argues that God does not require this.

"For his eyes are upon the ways of a man,
  and he sees all his steps.

There is no gloom or deep darkness
   where evildoers may hide themselves.
For he has not appointed a time for any man
   to go before God in judgment.
He shatters the mighty without investigation,
   and sets others in their place" (vv. 21–24).

God does not need to hold a trial to condemn us
or set us aside if we are misbehaving. He knows
immediately what is going on; he sees the depths
of the heart and he understands the thoughts of the
mind. Read Psalm 139 and see how the psalmist mar-
vels at God's ability to understand his thoughts from
afar—even before they take shape in his mind and
heart. Elihu goes on:

"Thus, knowing their words,
   he overturns them in the night, and they are crushed.
He strikes them for their wickedness
   in the sight of men,
because they turned aside from following him . . ."
                                      3 4 (vv. 25–27).

This is the issue, "They turned aside from following him." That is the standard of performance which
God righteously expects of men. How hard it is for
us to learn that the only way we can properly relate
to life is to begin with God. He holds the world in
his grasp. Excluding God from our life is totally un-
realistic living. Those who turned aside from him,

". . . and had no regard for any of his ways,
   so that they caused the cry of the poor to come to him,
   and he heard the cry of the afflicted" (vv. 27, 28),

simply have shown that they do not want God. God
judges them for that defection when it results in

cruelty and affliction. There is no other standard acceptable to him. In verses 29 and 30 Elihu goes on:

"When he is quiet, who can condemn?
  When he hides his face, who can behold him,
    [How are you going to summon God to a trial and make
    him speak?]
    whether it be a nation or a man?—
that a godless man should not reign,
  that he should not ensnare the people."

Again Elihu asks, who can call God to account or appeal his decision? There is no way man can do this, nor is there any need to do it because God is always consistent with himself. Thus Elihu concludes with the statement, in effect, that God accepts no substitute for righteousness. These words are somewhat confused in the Hebrew text and therefore the English is not too clear. Perhaps the *New English Bible* puts it a little more clearly:

"But suppose you will say to God,
'I have overstepped the mark, I will do no more mischief.
Vile wretch that I am, be thou my guide;
whatever wrong I have done, I will do no more.'
Will he, at those words, condone your rejection of him?
It is for you to decide, not me:
but what can you answer?" (vv. 31–33).

Good question, isn't it? What he is pointing out is that someone may say, "Well, all right, I got into trouble, I did something wrong but I won't do it anymore. I'll reform my life and watch in that area, but I'm still going to run my life myself." Elihu says, "Can you say that to God? He will not accept that." Reform is not what he is after; God desires repentance and relationship, the surrender of the right to run your life, and he will accept no other basis of relationship.

Now Elihu closes with God's problem concerning Job:

> "Men of understanding will say to me,
>   and the wise man who hears me will say:
> 'Job speaks without knowledge,
>   his words are without insight.'
> Would that Job were tried to the end,
>   because he answers like wicked men.
> For he adds his rebellion to his sin;
>   he claps his hands among us,
>   and multiplies his words against God" (vv. 34–37).

What Elihu is saying is that Job is obviously speaking out of ignorance of the nature and the true character of God, and therefore he needs further treatment. "Would that Job were tried to the end," he says— not because this young man wants to increase his agony, but because only that will bring Job to the truth—so he asks that it go on until Job sees what he is doing.

The Toughest Lesson

Job is a righteous man, his heart is right, he wants to serve God, but he thinks he can do it by his own efforts. The toughest lesson God has to teach us is to see the evil in what we think is nothing but good. We invariably think that our efforts to obey the truth as we understand it are totally acceptable to God. The hardest lesson of life is to learn that our righteousness is but filthy rags in his sight! It is only our dependence on his *gift* of righteousness that will ever be acceptable to him.

Here is the struggle of Romans 7 cropping up in the Old Testament. In Romans 7, Paul, whose heart was right, desired to do what God wanted and was trying his best to do it. Instead it all fell apart, and he cried out, "Wretched man that I am! Who will deliver me?" Then the word of faith comes in: "It is the gift of God. You are righteous, not by trying, but by accepting what God has said, by claiming his gift of righteousness through Jesus Christ, our Lord."

Remember that it was God who initiated this contest, not Satan. God said to Satan, "Notice my friend Job here? See what you can do with him." God had something to teach this man, and it is the same truth he is teaching many of us. When we think our behavior is absolutely right before him we have failed to grasp the one basis upon which we can truly be right. That is often why trouble comes to us. It alone will teach us the ugliness of self-righteousness.

We can move through these next three chapters very quickly. In detail Elihu now answers Job's ignorant argument. First, he restates it:

And Elihu said:
"Do you think this to be just?
Do you say, 'It is my right before God,'
that you ask, 'What advantage have I?'
How am I better off than if I had sinned?' " (vv. 1–3).

This is what Job has been saying: "God is unjust, I might as well have gone out and lived like the rest of them. Why should I have kept myself clean? I might as well have been as mean and dirty and vicious and self-centered as anyone else." This is a common argument with us, as though the purpose of being righteous is to be blessed by God. But now Elihu examines that. First, he says to Job, "You're very inconsistent."

"Look at the heavens, and see;
    and behold the clouds, which are higher than you"

                                                    (v. 5).

That is, you cannot do anything to them. They are up there floating along, and you cannot even reach them. So, he says, it is like that with God:

"If you have sinned, what do you accomplish against him?
    and if your transgressions are multiplied, what do
    you do to him?
If you are righteous, what do you give to him;
    or what does he receive from your hand?
Your wickedness concerns a man like yourself,
    and your righteousness a son of man" (vv. 6–8).

In other words, "God is unaffected, no matter how you react. He is not acting toward you out of spite, out of personal anger at you. What you do or do not do does not change God or affect him in any way. Therefore, how can your actions make him act unjustly, as you say? God will be God no matter what you do." Job's argument, therefore, is toally inconsistent.

Crying for Relief

But then Elihu goes on, in a most helpful passage, to show us why God does appear to be indifferent to us, and why he does often appear to be insensitive to what happens to us:

"Because of the multitude of oppressions people cry out;
   they call for help because of the arm of the mighty.
But none says, 'Where is God my Maker,
   who gives songs in the night,
who teaches us more than the beasts of the earth,
   and makes us wiser than the birds of the air?'
There they cry out, but he does not answer,
   because of the pride of evil men" (vv. 9–12).

Why is God silent? Men cry for help, but God knows that what they are crying for is merely relief. They want to be delivered from the painful effects of their selfish ways but then allowed to go right back to being selfish. No one is concerned about God's glory, about being taught by God. Rather, they are simply crying out for deliverance; they want to use God. To that kind of appeal God is silent. This is often why our prayers are unanswered. Our selfishness has produced agony in our life and all we want is to escape the penalty; we are not at all concerned about God himself. That is one reason for God's silence.

Then Elihu points out another reason, in Job's conduct:

"Surely God does not hear an empty cry,
   nor does the Almighty regard it.
How much less when you say that you do not see him,
   that the case is before him, and you are waiting for him!"
                                        (vv. 13, 14).

This is a reference to Job's words about wanting to come to trial before God; that he would be his own defense attorney and would prove he was in the right and God's treatment of him was unjust. Elihu says, "How can you say that to God? Do you think God is really waiting for you to prove him wrong?" In verses 15 and 16 he goes on:

"And now, because his anger does not punish,
    and he does not greatly heed transgression,
Job opens his mouth in empty talk,
    and he multiplies words without knowledge."

How faithful this young man is to put it as gently as he can; he speaks the truth in love. He says, "Job, the problem is you want to prove that God is wrong and you are right. How can God respond to that? He doesn't punish you for it, he is patient with you, he doesn't strike you down when you talk that way, but you have taken advantage of his patience to speak words that are without knowledge; you speak out of ignorance."

Then, in chapters 36 and 37, we have a great revelation of the glory of God. Notice that it begins with Elihu's claim to speak with divine authority:

And Elihu continued, and said:
"Bear with me a little, and I will show you,
    for I have yet something to say on God's behalf.
I will fetch my knowledge from afar [i.e., it is not coming from me],
    and ascribe righteousness to my Maker" (vv. 1–3).

That is the place to start in all human reasoning. God is right, and therefore anything that deviates from what he says is wrong. Do not start with, "I'm right because I feel this way." That is what gets us into trouble. Start with, "God is right, and I must agree with him." That is where Elihu starts:

"For truly my words are not false;
    one who is perfect in knowledge is with you" (v. 4).

Some of the commentators have thought that he means himself, and surely this would be a brash and arrogant statement. But this is not what he means. If you refer ahead to chapter 37, verse 16, you will notice to whom he refers when he says, "one who is perfect in knowledge." There he asks Job,

"Do you know the balancings of the clouds,
　the wondrous works of him who is perfect in knowledge. . . ?"

Obviously he means God. Therefore, his claim in chapter 36 is that he is speaking with the wisdom and the knowledge of God. He speaks, not from himself, but by means of the Spirit.

In verses 5 through 15 he declares that God is both merciful and just:

"Behold, God is mighty, and does not despise any;
　he is mighty in strength of understanding.
He does not keep the wicked alive,
　but gives the afflicted their right" (vv. 5, 6).

God demonstrates his mercy and justice, first, by his treatment of kings:

". . . then he declares to them their work and
　their transgressions" (v. 9).

". . . He opens their ears to instruction" (v. 10).

"If they hearken and serve him,
　they complete their days in prosperity" (v. 11).
"But if they do not hearken, they perish by the sword"
(v. 12).

Then God demonstrates his justice by his treatment of the proud. Once again we have a passage

(v. 13, 14) that is rather confused in the English. Here it is from the *New English Bible:*

> "Proud men rage against him
> and do not cry to him for help when caught in his toils;
> So they die in their prime,
> like male prostitutes, worn-out."

Proud men wear themselves out against the greatness and the power of God, and die in their prime, like male prostitutes, worn-out. Surely there is nothing more pathetic than the middleaged homosexual! That leads Elihu to show how God uses affliction:

> "He delivers the afflicted by their affliction,
> and opens their ear by adversity" (v. 15).

Is God trying to get your attention by some pain or adverse circumstance, some pressure you are going through? He is opening your ear. He wants you to listen to what he is saying to you.

Job's Perilous Position

The account goes on to give a vivid description of Job's perilous position which this young man points out in faithfulness:

> "He also allured you out of distress
> into a broad place where there was no cramping, and what
> was set on your table was full of fatness.
> [God has blessed you, Job, in the past.]
> But you are full of the judgment on the wicked;
> judgment and justice seize you.
> [You're preoccupied with justice, here, as though that
> were the ground on which you could stand before God.]

Beware lest wrath entice you into scoffing;
  and let not the greatness of the ransom turn you aside"
  (vv. 16–18).

That comes out somewhat confused in the Hebrew
language. The Authorized Version is better here:

"Because there is wrath, beware lest he take thee away with
his stroke; then a great ransom cannot deliver thee."

Then Elihu concludes the section by warning Job:

"Will your cry avail to keep you from distress,
  or all the force of your strength?
Do not long for the night,
  when peoples are cut off in their place.
Take heed, do not turn to iniquity,
  for this you have chosen rather than affliction"
  (vv. 19–21).

His final word to Job is a great and beautiful passage in which he set forth the glory of God. It extends
from verse 22 through chapter 37. Let us take just
the highlights of it. First, God is beyond men's instruction:

"Behold, God is exalted in his power;
  who is a teacher like him?" (v. 22).

Then another "behold" in verse 26: God is beyond
men's understanding.

"Behold, God is great, and we know him not;
  the number of his years is unsearchable."

Still another "behold" in verse 30 and 31. God acts
beyond men's rigid categories and reasons.

> "Behold, he scatters his lightning about him,
>   and covers the roots of the sea.
> For by these [by storm and lightnings] he judges peoples;
>   he gives food in abundance."

God uses his natural powers for both blessing and judgment.

The Thunder of His Voice

Beginning with chapter 37, we have a marvelous description of a great electric storm. Many commentators feel that a storm actually began to break out at this moment and Elihu used it as a vivid example of what he had been saying about God. If you have ever been on the prairies during an electric storm you will know what a terrifying and awe-inspiring experience it is, with the lightning crackling and splitting the sky and the roaring of the thunder. This is what Elihu begins to describe:

> "At this also my heart trembles,
>   and leaps out of its place.
> Hearken to the thunder of his voice
>   and the rumbling that comes from his mouth.
> Under the whole heaven he lets it go,
>   and his lightning to the corners of the earth.
> After it his voice roars;
>   he thunders with his majestic voice
>   and he does not restrain the lightnings when his voice is
>   heard" (37:1-4).

He goes on to speak of the fact that God sends the snow and the rain. He sends tornadoes, whirlwinds and frost; he controls the cycles of the weather. Next time you are watching a weather report on television and they show you the satellite picture, notice how it appears in spirals. The weather comes in cycles, and this is what he refers to in verse 12:

> "They turn round and round by his guidance
>   to accomplish all that he commands them
>   on the face of the habitable world."

And then he tells us why:

> "Whether for correction, or for his land,
>   or for love, he causes it to happen" (v. 13).

God has many reasons for doing things and we are not always certain what they are. God's wisdom is inscrutable. Elihu goes on,

> "Do you know how God lays his command upon them . . ."
> (v. 15)?

> "Do you know the balancings of the clouds . . ." (v. 16)?

> "Can you, like him, spread out the skies . . ." (v. 18)?

Job can do none of these things. Job cannot explain them (vv. 14–16); Job cannot duplicate them (vv. 17, 18); Job cannot command them (vv. 19, 20).

Elihu closes with a beautiful picture of the matchless majesty of God:

> "Out of the north comes golden splendor;
>   God is clothed with terrible majesty.
> The Almighty—we cannot find him;
>   he is great in power and justice,
>   and abundant righteousness he will not violate.
> Therefore men fear him;
>   he does not regard any who are wise in their own conceit"
> (vv. 22–24).

All through the Bible, the only man or woman who ever receives anything from God is the one who comes with a humble and contrite heart. If you think you have something to offer him, or that you have accomplished achievements that no one else can equal, you cut yourself off from the wisdom and knowledge of God. But the man who is humble and contrite, waiting upon God, asking him to teach him, will find that God will lift him up in grace and power and glory.

That is what is about to happen to Job. The very next voice we hear, as chapter 38 opens, will be the voice of God himself, speaking directly to Job.

Father, our hearts are humble as we see how mighty are your ways. We pray that, if nothing else, this great book will teach us the majesty and the glory and the wonder of our God. What a marvelous Being you are, Lord. Help us to take the place of the learner and be taught out of humility and weakness, that we might be strong, because of the grace of our loving God. Teach us, Lord, to accept what comes from your hand, knowing that you will take us through the struggles and bring us out into a broad and wonderful place, as you did Job. We ask in Jesus' name, Amen.

10

The God of Nature

In chapters 38 to 41 we reach the climax of this great Book of Job. Here the voice of Jehovah himself is heard, speaking out of the whirlwind. There are other places in the Scriptures where God symbolizes his presence by a wind. Jesus said to Nicodemus, "The Spirit of God is like the wind. It is sovereign, it blows where it will. Except a man be born of wind and water he cannot enter into the kingdom of God." Jesus here used two symbols—the wind for the Spirit of God, and water, for the Word of God. To be born again requires both the Word and the Spirit of God. On the day of Pentecost God turned on a mighty, rushing wind, which, like a great siren, brought the whole city to the temple courts to see the strange phenomenon taking place there: men speaking in other tongues with dancing flames of fire upon their heads. Wind is thus a frequent symbol in Scripture for God. Out of the whirling wind the voice of God comes:

Then the Lord answered Job out of the whirlwind:
"Who is this that darkens counsel by words without knowl-
   edge?
Gird up your loins like a man,
   I will question you, and you shall declare to me"

                                                    (38:1–3).

Certain of the commentators have thought that
these words were addressed to Elihu, but at the end
of the book Job applies these words to himself. It
is clear therefore that God is speaking here to Job.
God challenges Job who, by his ignorant words, has
been darkening the light that could have come to
him. How many times have we done the same thing?
God may be speaking to us but we have darkened
the light by ignorant words of complaint, rebuke
and rebellion against his will.

Now Jehovah demands of Job, "Gird up your loins
like a man and let me ask you some questions. You
have claimed that you want a trial before me. Well,
let me examine your competence. See if you can
answer some simple questions first." He indicates
that the questions will be those a man should be
able to answer. God's great discourse runs through
chapters 38 to 41. He subjects Job to a series of penetrating questions in three different areas. First, he
examines Job's knowledge of creative wisdom exhibited in the world and in the heavens. Then God
turns to the theme of his providential care of the
animal creation, and finally, he explores his restraint
of the forces of evil at work in the world.

Where Were You?

Jehovah introduces this with a series of questions
about the foundations of the earth:

"Where were you when I laid the foundation of the earth?
    Tell me, if you have understanding.
Who determined its measurements—surely you know!
    Or who stretched the line upon it?
On what were its bases sunk,
    or who laid its cornerstone,
when the morning stars sang together,
    and all the sons of God shouted for joy?" (vv. 4–7).

There is no more magnificent poetry in all the world than this section of the Book of Job. Here God calls Job's attention to the bases upon which the earth itself rests. He calls them the foundations of the earth and challenges Job to explain them. Notice how simply he puts the questions. These are but kindergarten questions. They come in terms of "Where, who, what, and when?" First, "Where were you, when I laid the foundation of the earth?" Where *was* man? He was not even in existence yet. In all the centuries since this question was asked of Job, man has never been able to settle the question of origins. Where did the universe come from? Who brought it into being? What process was followed? The scientific world is debating that question today, but man has never been able to answer it because he was not there to observe it.

Then in verse 5 the Almighty implies that someone helped him in this:

"Who determined its measurements—surely you know!
    Or who stretched the line upon it?"

There is at least a hint here that someone assisted him in this work. Recall that the Gospel of John begins:

In the beginning was the Word, and the Word was with God, and the Word was God . . . all things were made through him, and without him was not anything made that was made.

There we learn that the Trinity was at work in creation. In this question to Job there is a hint that God the Father was not alone in this work, that other members of the Trinity were involved with it as well.

In verse 6 there is a question of procedure. How did God hang the earth upon nothing, as Job himself put it earlier in this account? In the days when the Scriptures were being written down, the scientific world of that time believed that the earth was flat. There were strange, legendary accounts of how the earth came into being, that it floated on elephants' backs, or rested on turtles swimming in the sea. But in the Book of Job we have the clear statement that God has hung the earth upon nothing. Now God asks Job, "How did that happen?" The only answer science can give today is gravity, but no one really knows what gravity is. It is just a word we use, but it does not tell us what it is. This is a question that we still cannot answer today. How is the earth suspended between the various heavenly bodies in such a way that it moves in orderly procession through the illimitable reaches of space? How can it be?

Finally, God says, "Were you there when it happened?" and he links it with the tremendous reaction of the whole creation which seemed to break into harmony and melody, "when the morning stars sang together, and all the sons of God shouted for joy."

The Oceans Were Born

Then God turns to the most prominent feature on the earth, the sea. If you look at pictures of the earth as it is seen from space you will see that three-quarters of the globe is covered with water. God employs a beautiful symbolism here, as though the oceans suddenly were born, like a baby springing forth from the womb.

"Or who shut in the sea with doors,
   when it burst forth from the womb;
when I made clouds its garment,
   and thick darkness its swaddling band,
and prescribed bounds for it,
   and set bars and doors,
and said, 'Thus far shall you come, and no farther,
   and here shall your proud waves be stayed'?" (vv. 8–11).

We know that water is made up of two invisible gases, hydrogen and oxygen, and when these two are combined, a visible substance, water, springs into being. What a dramatic moment when God caused these invisible gases to join together in such quantities that an ocean suddenly spread across this planet! God asks Job about it, but Job knows nothing at all concerning it.

The emphasis of this section seems to be on how the ocean is controlled. God said he set its bounds and said to it, "Thus far shall you come, and no farther, and here shall your proud waves be stayed." It has always seemed to me symbolic of the ways of God that the substance he uses to keep the ocean in its bed, sand, is one of the most shifting, unreliable substances known. Beaches of sand hold the oceans in place and say, "Thus far shall you come."

Then, in the next verses, Jehovah examines Job on some of the secret processes of earth. First, on the matter of day and night:

> "Have you commanded the morning since your days began,
>   and caused the dawn to know its place,
> that it might take hold of the skirts of the earth,
>   and the wicked be shaken out of it?
> It is changed like clay under the seal,
>   and it is dyed like a garment.
> From the wicked their light is withheld,
>   and their uplifted arm is broken" (vv. 12–16).

God describes here how the sun rises in a different place every morning, changing according to the seasons, moving from north to south. His question is, "Have you caused the dawn to know its place? Are you able to tell the sun just where to get up so that it marks the exact season of the year?" Then he says, "Are you able to control the effect of light upon society?" Light "takes hold of the skirts of the earth," he says.

Have you ever seen the sun coming up and noticed how the fingers of light seemed to lay hold of the darkness and dissipate it? This imagery speaks of the wicked hiding from the light and then going back into their dens. Then as the day goes on, the sun, rising and coursing across the heavens, changes the colors of things. We know how scenery is altered by the different positions of the sun through the day. In the evening hours, when redness spreads across the sky, what a different cast it puts upon things. God is asking Job, "Can you do this? Are you able to change it like this?" Finally, "Can you control the length of time that darkness prevails (when the wicked operate) and stop them in their deeds (when the daylight comes again)?" Thus, "their uplifted arm is broken."

Then he speaks of the deep things of the earth:

"Have you entered into the springs of the sea,
   or walked in the recesses of the deep?" (v. 16).

It is remarkable that we are only now beginning to plumb and map some of the deep places of the sea. The secrets of the deep are still largely hidden to us.

God then asks, "How about realms beyond life, Job? Can you understand that?"

"Have the gates of death been revealed to you,
   or have you seen the gates of deep darkness?" (v. 17).

Death is still an unsolved mystery to us. Science is unable to help us here.

Verse 18 presents perhaps the one question out of all this list we can answer today:

"Have you comprehended the expanse of the earth?
   Declare, if you know all this."

"Do you know what is the extent of the surface of the globe?" Today, perhaps, we can say yes. We have mapped most of the earth—not all of it—but it has almost all been explored. Thus, thousands of years after Job we have come to an answer on that. It is possible to take a jet plane in London, have lunch in New York and dinner in San Francisco, and, of course, pick up your baggage in Buenos Aires! We have covered the expanse of the earth at last, even though there are still some areas we do not know much about. But how long it has taken to solve even one of these simple problems that Job was asked about!

God goes on into other mysteries, the common things of life:

> "Where is the way to the dwelling of light,
>   and where is the place of darkness,
> that you may take it to its territory
>   and that you may discern the paths to its home?
> You know, for you were born then
>   and the number of your days is great!" (vv. 19–21).

God heaps irony on Job. What he is asking, basically, is, "Do you understand how light is produced?" Once again, the scientific world is baffled even today by that. Two conflicting theories try to explain how light emerges, how it suddenly comes into being, but no one really knows. We cannot yet "take it to its territory and discern the paths to its home." We are unable to solve even that simple process.

> "Have you entered the storehouses of the snow,
>   or have you seen the storehouses of the hail,
> which I have reserved for the time of trouble,
>   for the day of battle and war?" (vv. 22, 23).

These are among the most intriguing verses in all of the Scriptures. For years I have wondered what they refer to. They suggest there is some hidden process in the formation of snow and hail—the process of vaporizing or freezing or whatever it may be—that will release tremendous power, which God says man will discover in the time when the whole of the earth is engaged in war. Something is hidden there. I have asked scientists about it and they shake their heads and say they do not know what that means. God says, "I have reserved it for the time of trouble." In Scripture that almost always refers to the last days, the terrible time of Jacob's trouble, when the great tribulation bursts upon the earth.

The Sun's Effect

Can you imagine what Job must be feeling like by now? All these questions are coming and he has not answered one correctly yet! Then God goes on:

"What is the way to the place where the light is distributed,
    or where the east wind is scattered upon the earth?
Who has cleft a channel for the torrents of rain,
    and a way for the thunderbolt,
to bring rain on a land where no man is,
    on the desert in which there is no man;
to satisfy the waste and desolate land,
    and to make the ground put forth grass?
Has the rain a father,
    or who has begotten the drops of dew?" (vv. 24–28).

Here Jehovah is examining the forces in the common phenomenon of a storm, and he asks, "Do you understand this, Job?" Many scholars have been puzzled by the way this section begins. The question is, "What is the way to the place where the light is distributed?" For years people have wondered why God begins with light being distributed, but at last we have begun to get a clue as to what this may mean, for now the scientific world knows that all energy comes to us from the sun. The rays of the sun, broken into various wavelengths, activate all the processes in the world around us. Energy

comes from the sun and it produces various phenom-
ena, including the evaporation of water and the formation of clouds. It produces thunder and great bolts
of lightning. All this is distributed, ultimately, from
the rays of the sun. It is amazing how much is revealed here that we have painfully worked out after
thousands of years of scientific endeavor.

Then God speaks of the way he takes care of the
desert. "Who cares for the desert?" Have you ever
flown the entire width of this country from coast
to coast? Although we think of this as a heavily popu-
lated country, there are hundreds of thousands of
acres of desert. "Who cares for that?" God asks. Who
brings the rain to cause the desert to bring forth
blossoms that no man ever sees but God alone? As
the poet says,

Full many a rose is born
    to blush unseen
And waste its sweetness
    On the desert air.

The only answer, of course, is that God does this.
Man does not think of those things. He has a hard
enough time handling his own problems, let alone
taking care of the deserts of the earth.

Then God asks, "Has the rain a father, or who
has begotten the drops of dew?" Science now knows
that the rain does have a father. Before rain can
form into drops there must be dust in the air and
raindrops form around these little specks of dust.
That is why we spray the clouds with certain substances to try to increase the rainfall, because we
know now that the rain has a father.

Then, in verses 29 and 30, we have Jehovah's questions about the frost:

"From whose womb did the ice come forth,
　and who has given birth to the hoarfrost of heaven?
The waters become hard like stone,
　and the face of the deep is frozen."

Who understands the processes by which ice is formed? We see it happen but no one has ever been able to answer the question why water, when it freezes, does something that hardly any other substance on earth does. Instead of contracting, like other substances, water expands when it freezes. That simple fact makes life possible on earth. God is asking some very penetrating questions. For him they are the simple ABC's of life, but Job is unable to answer them.

Influence of the Stars

Now the Almighty turns to explore the heavens. First, the stellar heavens:

"Can you bind the chains of the Pleiades,
　or loose the cords of Orion?
Can you lead forth the Mazzaroth in their season,
　or can you guide the Bear with its children?
Do you know the ordinances of the heavens?
　Can you establish their rule on the earth?" (vv. 31–33).

From the very beginning of time men have known that in some strange way the stars affect the earth. No one has ever been quite able to analyze it. Many wild guesses have been made, and many strange so-called sciences have emerged from it, such as astrology, which insists that every human life is governed by what the stars do. Many people read their horoscopes every day to see what the stars have said they can do that day.

But that is not what God is asking about here. He is saying, "What about the influence the stars seem to have upon the seasons?" The Pleiades, that little circle of stars high in the heavens, appears in the springtime; it ushers forth the spring. What God is asking here is, "Can you bring the spring out in its season?" Orion is the mighty hunter who strides across the winter skies. God asks Job, "Can you produce winter, in its season?"

Then he says, "Can you lead forth the Mazzaroth?" It is a bit doubtful as to what that word means, but many think it refers to the constellations that make up the zodiac. He is asking, "Can you control the zodiac and its influence upon the affairs of men?" The Bear is what we call the "Great Dipper," and it points unerringly to the north. (If you stay up all night in the open and observe the stars, you will see them wheel in an endless circle around the north.) In Scripture the north is often seen as the seat of God, so that the whole universe seems to revolve around his throne. Job is being questioned here as to how much he understands about this.

Even today, astronomers understand little about these things. There are mysterious objects in space we know nothing about. These great "black holes" are to us a puzzling, mysterious phenomenon that we have not begun to understand. So we cannot go much further than Job in answering these questions.

Verses 34 to 38 cover the atmospheric heavens:

"Can you lift up your voice to the clouds,
    that a flood of waters may cover you?

Can you send forth lightnings, that they may go
  and say to you, 'Here we are'?
Who has put wisdom in the clouds,
  or given understanding to the mists?
Who can number the clouds by wisdom?
  Or who can tilt the waterskins of the heavens,
when the dust runs into a mass
  and the clods cleave fast together?"

When you have a drought and you desperately need rain, who can say to the heavens, "Rain!" and it will come? During a period of drought, God shows us the impotence of man and science to solve some of the most fundamental problems of life.

Who Feeds the Animals?

Now in the last three verses (which really belong with chapter 39), God turns to his providential care of the animal world. He begins by saying that he supplies food for them:

"Can you hunt the prey for the lion,
  or satisfy the appetite of the young lions,
when they crouch in their dens,
  or lie in wait in their covert?
Who provides for the raven its prey,
when its young ones cry to God,
  and wander about for lack of food?" (vv. 39–41).

What do you think we would do if God suddenly gave us the responsibility of feeding the animal world, as well as ourselves? When you consider the mess we are making of welfare today, can you imagine how much worse it would be if all the animals had to stand in line for food stamps? Can you see them, shivering and dying, waiting for the red tape of bureaucracy to loosen its eternal grip before they get anything to eat? God is saying to Job, "Can you handle that sort of thing?" No, he cannot. Yet the animals exist and have been fed for centuries. They prosper and increase when man is out of the picture. God preserves the species; it is man who wipes them out.

So Jehovah goes on, "What about obstetrical care for the animals?"

> "Do you know when the mountain goats bring forth?
>   Do you observe the calving of the hinds?
> Can you number the months that they fulfil,
>   and do you know the time when they bring forth,
>   when they crouch, bring forth their offspring,
>   and are delivered of their young?
> Their young ones become strong, they grow up in the open;
>   they go forth, and do not return to them" (39:1–4).

"Can you handle that? Do you have a Blue Cross plan for the animal world, to take care of them when they give birth?" No! Job has to hang his head again. He does not know anything about it, and neither do we.

God then takes up the varied nature of the animal world. He examines the wide-ranging freedom of the wild ass:

> "He scorns the tumult of the city;
>   he hears not the shouts of the driver.
> He ranges the mountains as his pasture,
>   and he searches after every green thing" (vv. 7, 8).

God is asking, "Who made animals to have these distinctive natures and to be driven by such powerful instincts that they will invariably do what they were made to do, and yet not be like other animals in this regard? Who gave them those instincts?" That is the question Job faces.

God speaks then of the wild ox:

"Is the wild ox willing to serve you?
Will he spend the night at your crib?
Can you bind him in the furrow with ropes,
or will he harrow the valleys after you?
Will you depend on him because his strength is great,
and will you leave to him your labor?
Do you have faith in him that he will return,
and bring your grain to your threshing floor?" (vv. 9–12).

The untameable nature of certain animals is given to them by God, and man can neither explain it nor change it.

Then he speaks of the stupidity of the ostrich, and God himself takes the blame for it. This is, I think, one of the most humorous passages in scripture:

"The wings of the ostrich wave proudly;
but are they the pinions and plumage of love?
For she leaves her eggs to the earth,
and lets them be warmed on the ground,
forgetting that a foot may crush them,
and that the wild beast may trample them.
She deals cruelly with her young, as if they were not hers;
though her labor be in vain, yet she has no fear;
because God has made her forget wisdom,
and given her no share in understanding.
When she rouses herself to flee,
she laughs at the horse and his rider" (vv. 13–18).

An ostrich can outrun a horse, and yet it is so stupid that it walks off and leaves its eggs right out in the open! It will not take care of its young. But God says, "I like it that way, I made her like that." The

ostrich, the camel and other strange animals show
that God has a sense of humor. When I was in Austra-
lia I saw a duck-billed platypus, which looks like it
was put together from all the leftover spare parts
of creation. Why does God make animals like that?
I believe it is to show us certain characteristics of
our humanity.

In verses 19 to 25 we have a beautifully poetic
description of the courage of the horse:

> "Do you give the horse his might?
>   Do you clothe his neck with strength?
> Do you make him leap like the locust?
>   His majestic snorting is terrible.
> He paws in the valley, and exults in his strength;
>   he goes out to meet the weapons.
> He laughs at fear, and is not dismayed;
>   he does not turn back from the sword.
> Upon him rattle the quiver,
>   the flashing spear and the javelin.
> With fierceness and rage he swallows the ground;
>   he cannot stand still at the sound of the trumpet.
> When the trumpet sounds, he says, 'Aha!'
>   He smells the battle from afar,
>   the thunder of the captains, and the shouting."

From time immemorial man has used the horse
in battle because the horse has a unique character—
he loves conflict and competition. When I was a boy
in high school I had my own horse. He was a kind
of maverick, a short animal (his name was Shorty),
but he had an unconquerable spirit. He would never
let another horse get ahead of him. I had all I could
do to keep him under control when some other horse
tried to pass him. He would almost literally kill himself to get out in front, because he had such a compet-

itive spirit. He loved a race and wanted to be first in it. This is the nature of a horse. Now who made him that way? That is God's question.

Then he speaks of the hawk and the eagle, and of their strange ways, the keenness of their sight, and the fierceness of their character. Finally, he concludes with this question:

And the Lord said to Job:
"Shall a faultfinder contend with the Almighty?
He who argues with God, let him answer it" (40:1, 2).

"Are you able to argue, Job? How have you done in this examination? I have asked all these questions. How many have you got right? If you can't handle these little things, how are you going to press me on these great questions of what lies behind the strange experiences of life?"

Then Job answered the Lord:
"Behold, I am of small account; what shall I answer thee?
I lay my hand on my mouth.
I have spoken once, and I will not answer;
twice, but I will proceed no further" (vv. 3–5).

Job is silenced by this display of God's creative wisdom. What Job says is, basically, "I see that I am not in the same league as you are. I am of small account." Remember, earlier he had said, "If I could just come before the Lord, like a prince would I come before him. I would present my case and prove myself right." But now he says, "I'm not in the same league at all. I'm just small peanuts. I couldn't handle this." But he has not gone deep enough yet. Job is silenced, but he is not convinced. He has not yet seen what his basic problem is. He has not learned what God had in mind when he invited Satan to try him in the first place.

So in the next account Jehovah produces, by the use of symbols, a revelation of what he is doing in Job's life that will leave Job absolutely without an answer. By it he is humbled before God and falls on his face, waiting for God to deliver him and restore him—which he immediately does. But at this point he has only been silenced.

This often happens to us. Sometimes our troubles bring us to a place where we shut up. We stop complaining, but that is not what God wants. What he wants is for us to trust him, to put the matter back into his hands and believe that he is working things out right. God will show us in our next study why he has to do it this way.

Like Job, Father, we bow in silence before you. Who are we to accuse the Almighty? Who are we to charge you with injustice? Who are we to complain about our lot in life and say it is wrong, that we have been treated unfairly? Lord, we too have been silenced, but we pray that you will take us deeper even as you do Job, and in graciousness show to us mighty things that you are working out through the very circumstances of our lives that we never dreamed about. Help us to understand what is going on. We pray that we may bow before your majesty, and humbly ascribe to you the glory that is due your name. In Jesus' name, Amen.

11

The Nature of God

Life, as we grow older, has a way of overturning some of the convictions of our youth. Many of us have had the experience of looking back at what we stood for, and were absolutely certain was the right thing to do or the right attitude to have, which we now see to have been wrong. Carl Jung, the great Austrian psychologist, put it this way:

> In the second half of life the necessity is imposed of recognizing no longer the validity of our former ideals but of their contraries; of perceiving the error in what was previously our conviction; of sensing the untruth in what was our truth, and of weighing the degree of opposition, and even of hostility, in what we took to be love.

How many of us have learned that lesson! Looking back, we have seen that what we thought was an action of love was really a self-centered exhibition of our own pride and desire. That is what God is teaching Job now, helping him to see that his righteousness was an external matter only, and that internally there was a deep and serious problem.

God began by revealing his creative wisdom in all that he had made, in the manifold forces of nature, and he subjected Job to a penetrating examination on natural subjects. Job came to the end of the first session with his hand on his mouth: silenced, but not convinced.

Now Jehovah takes up the argument again, and in chapter 40, verses 6 through 8, he brings up another matter with Job:

> Then the Lord answered Job out of the whirlwind:
> "Gird up your loins like a man;
>   I will question you, and you declare to me.
> Will you even put me in the wrong?
>   Will you condemn me that you may be justified?"

God is still speaking out of the whirling wind, employing anew this great symbol of the Spirit's power. What an amazing experience it must have been to hear a voice coming out of a whirlwind! This time he brings another question before Job: "Can you handle the moral government of earth?" Job has already admitted that he is not in God's league when it comes to understanding the world of nature or caring for the animals. Now God says, "What about the moral realm? That is the very area in which you have been charging me with fault. Can you handle that? Are you able to put me in the wrong in this area of morality?"

Mount the Throne

Then, in the next section, he invites Job to mount the throne of God, as it were, to see what he would do with the problems God has to face:

"Have you an arm like God,
   and can you thunder with a voice like his?
Deck yourself with majesty and dignity;
   clothe yourself with glory and splendor.
Pour forth the overflowings of your anger,
   and look on every one that is proud, and abase him.
Look on every one that is proud, and bring him low;
   and tread down the wicked where they stand.
Hide them all in the dust together;
   bind their faces in the world below.
Then will I also acknowledge to you,
   that your own right hand can give you victory"

(vv. 9–14).

This is God's challenge now to Job: "Can you look and sound like God? Can you clothe yourself with majesty and dignity so that all the created universe is immediately aware of your power? Can you appear like God, and especially, can you handle the problem of the proud?" Now God puts his finger on the problem that is in Job's heart, though Job does not know it. "Can you handle the proud? Can you find a way to abase these proud, strutting creatures who think they have all that they need to handle life?"

We know in our day what a difficult problem this is. Here in our country we have an organization that everyone calls "the Mafia," made up of proud men who feel they have power to run life to please themselves. Basically, they are criminals. Parasites on society, they live for their own purposes and advance their own interests. They extract hundreds of thousands of dollars from innocent people. Yet the power of government and of our judicial system is unable to lay hold of these men and arrest them in their proud, selfish course. They remain almost untouched among us, decade after decade. It is not easy to run the earth. It is not easy to bring justice. God says,

"Can you do this, Job? Can you handle proud men and even, if necessary, consign them to the world below (i.e., to hades, or hell)? If you can, Job, then I will be willing to grant that you are able to handle your own problem and give yourself victory, as you claim you can."

Now God zeroes right in on the problem with Job. In the next sections he brings before us two amazing animals: one called "Behemoth," a land animal for the most part; and one called "Leviathan," a sea creature. Commentators have had a great deal of difficulty trying to determine just which animals in our natural world are referred to here. Some think the Behemoth is either the hippopotamus, or the elephant, or perhaps the rhinoceros. Leviathan is thought by some to be the crocodile, though others think it could be the whale.

For the most part it is a waste of time to argue about the identity of these animals. The language employed here clearly goes beyond the natural realm. In the last section, where God was taking Job through a tour of his created universe, all the animals were recognizable, though they were described in poetic language. But here we have something that goes beyond the natural. Therefore, some of the commentators have felt these are mythical, legendary creatures, like the unicorn and the dragon. But more likely these beasts are symbolic, spoken of as animals in the natural realm, but symbols of that which is invisible and supernatural.

Scripture has many examples of this sort of thing. In the books of Daniel, Zechariah, and Revelation, forces on earth are symbolized by beasts: beasts that rise up out of the sea and come up on the land. They symbolize movements and individuals and leaders, and even invisible and supernatural powers. Here we have another example of that. In fact, we are given help from some of the other scriptures to recognize these beasts. Isaiah 27 tells us plainly what Leviathan represents. In the opening verse Isaiah says,

> In that day [referring to the final day, the great day of the Lord] the Lord with his hard and great and strong sword will punish Leviathan the fleeing serpent, Leviathan the twisting serpent, and he will slay the dragon that is in the sea (27:1).

It is most interesting that the names of these beasts in Hebrew mean something very significant. *Behemoth* is the Hebrew word for "beasts" (plural). Not just *a* beast but all beasts, lumped together, are apparently symbolized by Behemoth; while *Leviathan* means "the folded one." You can see in that the description of a dragon, with the elongated body that is often represented as folded up, like a snake with its loops. In Isaiah 27 we are told very plainly that Leviathan is that twisting, folded serpent, also called "the dragon that is in the sea."

Two Beasts, One Power

Now your mind, I am sure, has already run ahead to the Book of Revelation, where in chapter 13 two beasts emerge that dominate the scene in the last days. One is a beast which comes up out of the sea, and that beast reigns over the waters which, we are told, represent the multitudes of peoples of the earth. The other beast comes up on the land. Behind both of these beasts is still a third incredible animal called the great dragon (of chapter 12). There we are told plainly that the dragon is Satan, and he gives his power and authority to the beasts. Now, applying this symbolism to the Book of Job, it appears that these beasts represent a satanic power made visible in terms of our earthly existence. The first of these beasts, Behemoth, represents the satanic twist that we all labor with and struggle against in our own lives, which the Bible calls "the flesh," the fallen nature within us—humanity, with its continual desire to assert itself and live for itself.

The second beast represents the world in its vast influence upon every one of us, pressuring us to conform, to reflect the values and attitudes of those around us, dominating all our thinking and our life in every possible way. Behind them both is the devil, the old Serpent, with his malevolent, cunning wisdom and power, incredible in his might and his control of human events. God is setting before Job a very pertinent question for all of us: "Are you able to handle the enemy within, and the enemy without, and especially that malicious being who is behind them all?" One biblical commentator, Mr. Wordsworth, puts it this way:

> It seems probable that Behemoth represents the evil one acting in the animal and carnal elements of man's own constitution, and that Leviathan symbolizes the evil one energizing as his external enemy (i.e., man's external enemy). Behemoth is the enemy within us; Leviathan is the enemy without us— the world, the flesh, and the devil.

Now, with that to guide us as we look at these two beings, let us see how God sets them before Job:

> "Behold, Behemoth,
>   which I made as I made you;
>   he eats grass like an ox.

Behold, his strength is in his loins,
  and his power in the muscles of his belly.
He makes his tail stiff like a cedar;
  the sinews of his thighs are knit together.
His bones are tubes of bronze,
  his limbs like bars of iron" (vv. 15–18).

Incredible strength! Total self-sufficiency! That is the picture here; Behemoth is so well adapted to its environment that it appears completely self-sufficient. The next verse is very interesting:

"He is the first of the works of God;
  let him who made him bring near his sword!"

That is another of those verses which in the original Hebrew language is difficult to understand. Perhaps another translation, from the *New English Bible,* would help us at this point. That version reads,

"He is the chief of God's works,
  made to be a tyrant over his peers!"

Here is an animal that stands for the desire to rule over everyone else. It is the picture of self-centeredness, that tyranny within us that wants to be in control of everything around.

Jehovah goes on:

"For the mountains yield food for him
  where all the wild beasts play.
Under the lotus plants he lies,
  in the covert of the reeds and in the marsh.
For his shade the lotus trees cover him;
  the willows of the brook surround him.
Behold, if the river is turbulent he is not frightened;
  he is confident though Jordan rushes against his mouth.
Can one take him with hooks,
  or pierce his nose with a snare?" (vv. 20–24).

The obvious conclusion to all those questions is: Here is a being so self-sufficient and so completely in control that he is filled with self-confidence no matter what happens to him. So we have symbolized the qualities of self-sufficiency, self-centeredness, and self-confidence. What better description could there be of the enemy within us, our inheritance from Adam, this independent spirit that says, "I don't need God or anyone else. I'm sufficient unto myself"?

We are all like this. We uphold this independent spirit. We glorify it in our movies and television. We hold it up before our young people as something to be aped and followed. We acclaim it as "the American way of life"! It is all characterized by self-reliance, self-centeredness, and self-confidence. We take courses to increase this spirit within us. Yet God says it is our enemy; it is what must be overcome.

The System Is Wrong

In chapter 41 the other animal, Leviathan, comes before us. The first was a land animal; this is a water animal, and the first thing God points out is his untameability:

"Can you draw out Leviathan with a fishhook,
  or press down his tongue with a cord?
Can you put a rope in his nose,
  or pierce his jaw with a hook?
Will he make many supplications to you?
  Will he speak to you soft words?
Will he make a covenant with you
  to take him for your servant for ever?
Will you play with him as with a bird,
  or will you put him on leash for your maidens?

Will traders bargain over him?
Will they divide him up among the merchants?" (vv. 1–6).

In the course of human history, who has ever been able to reform the world to make it serve the ends of humanity? The struggle of history is to make the world system, with all its many problems and relationships, its pride and its self-sufficiency, serve the ends of humanity. Every government, every administration, struggles with the same problems. No one has ever been able to master the world and its ways. Every generation of young people finds ways of expressing its revolt against "the system." This is the system described to us here. It lays its heavy hand of control upon us all and insists that we conform to its values and its illusions of what is important and profitable in life. We all live under this tremendous pressure, and find ourselves unable to resist it, just as it is described here.

God goes on to describe how unconquerable it is:

"Can you fill his skin with harpoons,
　or his head with fishing spears?
Lay hands on him;
　think of the battle; you will not do it again!
Behold, the hope of a man is disappointed;
　he is laid low even at the sight of him.
No one is so fierce that he dares to stir him up" (vv. 7–9).

Think back through history of all the proud world conquerors with their fierce spirit that would not brook opposition. How many times men have been afraid to oppose them! How invulnerable they appear, fulfilling in their day the proud symbol of world power.

In the second half of verse 10 and in verse 11, God interjects a parenthesis for Job to consider. "If you cannot handle this beast," he says,

> ". . . Who then is he that can stand before me?
> Who has given to me, that I should repay him?
> Whatever is under the whole heaven is mine."

God's argument is, "Job, if you cannot handle the scrub team, what are you going to do when the varsity plays?" Or as Jeremiah puts it, "If you faint and are weary when you run with the footmen, what are you going to do against horses?" God says, "I handle Leviathan all the time. He is my problem, and I can handle him. But Job, what are you going to do? If you cannot handle him, how do you ever hope to challenge me?" It is a good question for Job to consider.

Then God goes on to describe Leviathan further. He speaks of his ability to defend himself:

> "I will not keep silence concerning his limbs,
>   or his mighty strength, or his goodly frame.
> Who can strip off his outer garment?
>   Who can penetrate his double coat of mail?
> Who can open the doors of his face?
>   Round about his teeth is terror.
> His back is made of rows of shields,
>   shut up closely as with a seal.
> One is so near to another
>   that no air can come between them.
> They are joined one to another;
>   they clasp each other and cannot be separated"
> (vv. 12–17).

You can see why many have thought this was the crocodile, because of the description of the overlapping shields on his back and sides. But the next section goes far beyond the crocodile. It is obviously a picture of a deeply entrenched, well-defended system that cannot be overthrown.

Here we read of Leviathan's awesome fierceness and frightening power:

"His sneezings flash forth light,
  and his eyes are like the eyelids of the dawn.
Out of his mouth go flaming torches;
  sparks of fire leap forth.
Out of his nostrils comes forth smoke,
  as from a boiling pot and burning rushes.
His breath kindles coals,
  and a flame comes forth from his mouth.
In his neck abides strength,
  and terror dances before him.
The folds of his flesh cleave together,
  firmly cast upon him and immovable.
His heart is hard as a stone,
  hard as the nether millstone.
When he raises himself up the mighty are afraid;
  at the crashing they are beside themselves" (vv. 18–25).

What a picture of incredible strength and power—the great dragon breathing out flame from his nostrils and wiping out everything that comes against him!

Again we have a section on his invulnerability, how irresistible he is:

"Though the sword reaches him, it does not avail;
  nor the spear, the dart, or the javelin.
He counts iron as straw,
  and bronze as rotten wood.
The arrow cannot make him flee;
  for him slingstones are turned to stubble.

Clubs are counted as stubble;
   he laughs at the rattle of javelins.
His underparts are like sharp potsherds;
   he spreads himself like a threshing sledge on the mire"
                                   (vv. 26–30).

Then his power:

"He makes the deep boil like a pot;
   he makes the sea like a pot of ointment.
Behind him he leaves a shining wake;
   one would think the deep to be hoary" (vv. 31, 32).

Finally, the secret of his life, his pride:

"Upon earth there is not his like,
   a creature without fear.
He beholds everything that is high;
   he is king over all the sons of pride" (vv. 33, 34).

What a creature! What a being! This incredible beast is said to be king over all the sons of pride. He teaches men how to act in pride and independence and arrogance. He works it all into a vast system of control that lies over industry, labor, government, art and music, social and economic relationships of every kind. This is the beast that Job is up against. Now God's question is, "Job, are you able to handle this?" At last, God has brought Job to an awareness that these are the very things Job has in his own heart and life, and they describe forces over which he has no control.

At this point (though it is not stated in the account), God has made clear to Job what we were informed of at the very beginning of this book. Behind his sickness and his protracted agony lies an intense struggle with satanic power. We know that, but he does not. Now, at last, he is given a strong hint that the reason behind his illness is not his own failure or his own willful misdeeds, but a serious problem so embedded in his nature that he is not even aware that it exists—yet it is destroying him. This is what God has to deal with, and this is what he deals with in us.

God Is Right

Now we get Job's reaction.

Then Job answered the Lord:
"I know that thou canst do all things,
    and that no purpose of thine can be thwarted" (42:1, 2).

His first reaction is a new view of God himself. Notice the emphasis he makes here: "I know that thou canst do all things." God is omnipotent! Job knew that at the very beginning, but now he sees it expanded tremendously; and he also sees the sovereignty of God: "that no purpose of thine can be thwarted." Nothing that God plans ever sets aside man's responsibility. Yet nothing man ever chooses thwarts the purpose God intends to carry out. Isn't that amazing?

Job has now learned that God is a sovereign being, and that all he does is right. He is not only mighty, but he is right, acting always in line with his character of love. He is always consistent with himself. When Job sees God this way, he also sees himself rightly. This is always true. If we cannot understand ourselves it is because we do not know our God. When man loses God he always loses himself. When

man discovers God he finds himself. So Job now has
a new view of himself.

> " 'Who is this that hides counsel without knowledge?'
>   [He is quoting God's first address to him.]
> Therefore I have uttered what I did not understand,
> things too wonderful for me which I did not know.
> 'Hear, and I will speak;
>   I will question you, and you declare to me.'
>   [Here he is quoting God's second address to him.]
> I had heard of thee by the hearing of the ear,
>   but now my eye sees thee;
> therefore I despise myself,
>   and repent in dust and ashes" (vv. 3–6).

Notice the difference—"I had heard *of* thee by
the hearing of the ear, but now my eye *sees* thee."
The inner eye of Job's heart sees the nature of God.
And the result? Job says, "I despise myself." Now
that is repentance! What he is really doing is agreeing
with what God says about him. He quotes what God
says twice. He says, in effect, "Lord, you asked me,
'Who is this that hides counsel without knowledge?'
You are right, Lord. It is I. That is what I have been
doing. I am an ignorant man. I do not know enough
to challenge the wisdom of the Almighty. I am an
ignorant, limited man who speaks without even
knowing what he is talking about."

Then he quotes what God said to him again: "Hear,
and I will speak; I will question you, and you declare
to me." He is saying, "Lord, you are right about
that, too. I have been an arrogant man. I have been
thinking I could answer your questions, and that I
would even ask you questions that you could not
answer. Lord, I have been an arrogant man. I see
it now. Something within me has been proud, lifted

up, self-righteous, confident that I was right. I have been wrong all along." So, he says, "Lord, I despise myself."

Now it looks as though God has humiliated Job and cruelly brought this poor, broken-hearted man down into the dust. Yet it is not cruelty; it is love. For at this point, when Job has finally given up trying to defend and justify himself, God begins to heal him and to pour into his life blessing he never dreamed of.

This is the story of the whole of Scripture, isn't it? Jesus said, "Blessed are the poor in spirit [the men and women who are bankrupt in themselves, who stop counting on what they've got]. Blessed are the poor in spirit, *for theirs is the kingdom of heaven.*" God will begin to heal a life that repents before him and will fill it with blessing and honor and glory and power. None of the things we lose will be worth one tenth of the glory and joy we will discover in coming into a relationship with God himself. That is what we shall see in the closing section of Job. Here he is, confessing his sin, but also discovering the gift of forgiveness.

Thank you, our Father, for this searching and penetrating look at our own hearts and lives. How proud we have been, how filled with self-justification, with complaints before you, the living God. Lord, teach us to put our hand upon our mouth, and to do more than that, to admit to you that the problem lies with us, and put it back into your loving hands that by your redemptive grace, you will heal us and restore us. We thank you for the glorious gift of forgiveness. In Jesus' name, Amen.

12

The New Beginning

Jehovah has treated Job to a tour of the moral problems of the universe. Using the symbolism of two great beasts, Leviathan and Behemoth, God has shown him the depth of evil in humanity (what the New Testament calls "the mystery of lawlessness"), and why it is that every generation has to struggle with the same moral problems. We make no advance from century to century but wrestle with the same difficulties with which people wrestled thousands of years ago, even to the dawn of history. As Job learns the problems of his own heart, problems that God must deal with continually he bows his head before him. Before this breathtaking vision of God's power, wisdom and glory, Job repents in dust and ashes.

In chapter 42, at verse 7, we come to a new beginning. Job has learned his lesson. He thought he could trust God through any circumstance of life and was confident in his own ability to serve God. He is like Peter when he said to Jesus, "Everyone else will deny you but I will never do so. You can count on me." Quite honestly and earnestly from his heart, Job had been saying to God, "I'll stay with you no matter what." For a while he held out, but now God has shown him that without divine help he is totally weak and thoroughly undependable. Job has seen his guilt, repented, and confessed it before God.

A Hard Blow

Now it is the three friends' turn; Jehovah summons Eliphaz, the leader of the three. These friends were sitting by, silent, when Elihu came on the scene, but now God calls them before him:

> After the Lord had spoken these words to Job, the Lord said to Eliphaz the Temanite: "My wrath is kindled against you and against your two friends; for you have not spoken of me what is right, as my servant Job has. Now therefore take seven bulls and seven rams, and go to my servant Job, and offer up for yourselves a burnt offering; and my servant Job shall pray for you, for I will accept his prayer not to deal with you according to your folly; for you have not spoken of me what is right, as my servant Job has" (vv. 7, 8).

That sentence from God must have had a stunning effect upon Eliphaz and his two friends, for the one thing they had been sure of all through this account was that they were defending the righteousness of God. They were zealous for God's honor, upholding his sovereignty among men, and scathing in their denunciation of human pride and evil. Now, to their amazement, they are charged by God himself with defaming him. That must have been a hard blow to their pride.

What did they do that offended God so? You recall

that they formulated a theory of suffering in which
God was nothing but an arbitrator of justice, a great
cosmic judge, who visited punishment upon those
who did wrong, without exception and instantly. He
rewarded those who did right with prosperity and
blessing, also instantly. This was the kind of God
they set before people, a great judge of all men,
but not at all concerned with compassion, love,
mercy, and patience. Thus the God they talked about
was a God far from reality. They did indeed distort
the image of God.

Many Christians are like this. The God they present to people is wholly concerned with truth, as
though that is all there is, and deeply offended by
sin. They picture God as instantly responding to sin
with some kind of judgment. Their God is very stern
and harsh. Leaning over the battlements of heaven,
he is ready to cry, "Cut that out!" the minute anyone
steps out of line. As a result, the world gets a very
distorted view of what God is like. These three
friends meant to uphold God's righteousness, but
they said nothing about his mercy, his compassion,
his patience, his willingness to reach out to men and
wait for them to repent.

The Bible says that God sends the rain upon the
just and the unjust alike. God's blessings are not with-
held from those who are wrong and rebellious. He
gives them family life. He gives them joy, times of
pleasure, and times of peace. As Romans puts it, "the
goodness of God is designed to lead to repentance,"
that men may understand where their blessings are
coming from. God allows blessings to come in order
that we might turn to him as the basis of human
blessing and repent of our wickedness and our rebellion.

Then, looking back through the book, remember that these three also charged Job with hypocrisy, and even with outright wickedness, without any basis in fact whatsoever. They charged this man, who was normally upright in his conduct—even God himself said so—with being a hypocrite and with hiding some deep and terrible sin in his heart. In doing so, they represented themselves as the agents of God. God takes offense at that because they were actually doing the devil's work. The devil is the accuser of the brethren—the accuser in heaven and the destroyer on earth. Unwittingly, these men find themselves victims of the devil's lies, and they have become his instruments to torment Job. So God calls them to account. He says that his wrath is kindled against them because they have been guilty of these things.

He Wasn't All Wrong

Twice in this account God says that Job said what was right about him. We have never seen any recognition up to this time that Job had said anything right. In fact, the whole book points out that Job was wrong in his attitude about God. Although both the friends and Job say some wonderfully true things about God, yet now, Job himself has admitted that he spoke in ignorance and folly, and he repents of this and puts his hand upon his mouth. It is rather surprising then that God twice admits Job has said something right about him.

In what way did he say what was right? First, though Job indeed could see no sin in himself and did charge God with unfairness, yet the moment God showed him the sin deeply embedded in his heart, he immediately repented. There was no hesitation, no argument, no self-defense. He admitted immediately that the problem was in him and not in God.

Second, Job was always true to the facts as he saw them. He did not see them very clearly, and there are things about himself and about God's rule in the universe that he never understood—but he was always honest about what he could see. There was no distorting or twisting of the facts to fit an inadequate theology. He did not try to deceive himself, and he did not admit to things that he could not see were true.

Third, he took his problem to God, even though God was his problem. That is most admirable. All through the account he is constantly breaking into prayer. Despite the torment and anguish he feels, he always ends up laying his complaint before God. The three friends never pray for Job. They never ask God to relieve his suffering. They never ask God to give them wisdom or understanding. They simply ignore actual contact with the living God. But Job is forever crying out before God and bringing his problems unto the Lord himself and asking for wisdom and help. Jesus said to the people in his day, "Come unto me all ye that are weary and heavy laden, and I will give you rest." So Job finds rest in God.

Finally, when Job does repent, he declares without reservation that God is truly God, that he is holy and wise and just and good, even when he seems to be otherwise. Ultimately, that is the highest expression of faith—that we do not trust our human observations as to what is reality. We understand the limitations to our humanity and do not assume we have all the facts by which we can judge and condemn God. Job pronounces God to be just and holy in all that he does.

But to the credit of these three friends, they, too, immediately obey God when he tells them what is wrong:

> So Eliphaz the Teamanite and Bildad the Shuhite and Zophar the Naamanite went and did what the Lord had told them; and the Lord accepted Job's prayer (v. 9).

There is no resistance here either, no argument, even though it means they must go with their hat in their hand to Job, and ask him to pray for them. Can you imagine how humiliating that must have been, after all the proud things they had said against him; how they had put him down and scorned him? Now they must come and say, "Job, old friend, we're sorry for all we said. God has told us to ask you to pray for us." But they do it! They bring the offering of seven bulls and seven rams, as God had commanded.

In Scripture, seven is the number of perfection and the bull is the picture of service, so here is symbolized perfect service, even unto death. The ram in the Bible is the picture of energy, and seven rams offered symbolizes the total commitment of one's energies unto God, even unto death. In this burnt offering the friends are picturing the true basis of their acceptance before God—not their service and energy for him, but that which is represented by that great and all-sufficient substitute for man's wrongdoing, Jesus himself.

All the offerings of the Old Testament picture Christ. They are the way the Old Testament saints

looked ahead to the work of Christ, just as we look
back to the cross. As these men offered the bulls
and rams, it was an indication they understood that
before God, all man's honor is laid low and even
his best efforts are shown to be folly. They symboli-
cally turn from this to that perfect substitute for man,
the righteousness of Christ, and accept what God
gives in man's place.

It is natural for us to become angry with God when
he rejects our service, our efforts on his behalf. But
he labors to show us that nothing of human effort
can ever stand in his presence. The New Testament
tells us that "no flesh shall glory in his presence."
We must rest only on that sacrifice made on our
behalf, the righteousness of Christ himself.

No Pardon Without Prayer

Notice also God's insistence on intercessory prayer
here. What an interesting point this makes. God tells
these friends, "There will be no pardon for you without Job's petition on your behalf. If you want to be
received and forgiven you must not only bring the
sacrifices, but my servant Job must pray for you."
What an instructive lesson on prayer! Many of us
grow up with the idea that prayer is a way to manipu-
late God to do what we want—a kind of Heavenly
Aladdin's lamp that we can rub, sometimes for a
half-hour at a time, and expect God to suddenly appear as a genie and bow and say, "Master, what do
you want me to do for you?"

But prayer is not a way to get God to do what
we want. Prayer is the way God enlists us in what
he is doing. This is underscored here; it is so important God indicates that without prayer he will not

do anything. In the New Testament, James reminds us of Job when he tells us, "You have not because you ask not." How impoverished our lives are, and the lives of our friends and loved ones, simply because we think prayer is unimportant and do not bother to pray for one another. God underlines that importance here: "Your friends will not be accepted, Job, unless you pray for them." When Job prayed, they were indeed forgiven and pardoned.

Here is also a beautiful picture of forgiveness. Picture this scene in your imagination. Here is Job's chance, if he wanted it, to get even with these friends. When God sent them to him to ask for his prayers, how easy it would have been for him to say, "Aha! I thought you'd come around, you stinkers you! You were the ones who gave me all that trouble. You ran me down, you falsely accused me, you said all those evil things about me, and now I've got you where I want you. I'll let you sweat a bit. I'm going to get even with you!" That is what many of us would have said. But it is obvious that Job does not do so.

I wish we could have heard his prayer. I am sure it would have been something like this: "O Lord, here are these three friends of mine. They've been stubborn, hard-headed, foolish, ignorant men, just as I was, Lord. You forgave me, and now I ask you to forgive them as well." What a beautiful spirit of forgiveness must have been exercised here. Job might have continued, "I called them miserable comforters, and that's what they were. I suggested that they were so proud they thought they were the people, and wisdom would die with them. But Lord, I was just as proud and ignorant. You forgave me, and so, Lord, I ask you to forgive them as well." All we are told is that the Lord heard Job's prayer and accepted it, and the friends were forgiven.

This may well remind us of Paul's words in Ephesians 5, where he wrote to the Christians and said, "Be ye kind, tenderhearted one to another, forgiving one another, even as God for Christ's sake has forgiven you." I do not think there is anything more contrary to a Christian spirit than an unforgiving heart—to hold a grudge against someone else, or to refuse to talk to someone, or to be frosty in relationships with each other. What a beautiful thing it is to see Job praying for his friends, without a vestige of resentment or an attempt to get even, but holding them up before God. Then God honors that prayer, forgiving these men and restoring them to his grace, withholding his punishment, and blessing their lives.

In the next section, verses 10 through 13, we learn of the restoration that God brought into Job's life:

> And the Lord restored the fortunes of Job, when he had prayed for his friends; and the Lord gave Job twice as much as he had before. Then came to him all his brothers and sisters and all who had known him before, and ate bread with him in his house, and they showed him sympathy and comforted him for all the evil that the Lord had brought upon him; and each of them gave him a piece of money and a ring of gold. And the Lord blessed the latter days of Job more than his beginning; and he had fourteen yoke of oxen, and a thousand she-asses. He also had seven sons and three daughters.

James refers to this as "the purpose of the Lord," indicating it is what God had in mind for Job from the beginning and revealing God to be compassionate and merciful. Now, God did not suddenly become compassionate and merciful to Job; he has been that way all along. God's character, unchanging, is compassionate and merciful. He *is* love. This is what we must remember. Though he puts us through times of trial and pressures and hardships, as he did Job, it is not because he is angry and upset, it is because he is compassionate and merciful. If we wait, he will bring us to the place where we will see that as plainly and clearly as Job did. The purpose of the Lord is to reveal his heart of compassion and mercy to this dear old man.

There is a beautiful passage in Jeremiah's Lamentations that will help us greatly when we are going through trials and afflictions.

> For the Lord will not cast off forever, but though he cause grief, he will have compassion according to the abundance of his steadfast love, for he does not willingly afflict or grieve the sons of men (3:31–33).

Isn't that encouraging? He does not *willingly* afflict or grieve the sons of men. He will do it because he loves us and we need it, but he does not do it lightly. He feels with us in it. As a good parent with his children, he hurts worse than we do at times. "Though he cause grief, he will have compassion according to the abundance of his steadfast love."

Now God moves Job's relatives and friends to bring him gifts of silver and gold. Perhaps these gifts were God's way of providing a foundation of restored wealth for Job. At any rate, as the text tells us, Job ended up with double everything he had before. He started out with seven thousand sheep, and ended up with fourteen thousand. He had three thousand camels, and now he has six. He started out with five hundred yoke of oxen and now he has a thousand. He once had five hundred she-asses, but that is doubled now to one thousand. "Perhaps," you say, "God doubled everything but his sons and daughters. He ended up with only seven sons and three daughters, just like he had at the beginning." No, now he has seven sons and three daughters in heaven, and seven sons and three daughters more on earth; so God indeed gave Job double everything he had to start with. That is the mercy of God. He does not willingly afflict or grieve the sons of men, but longs to give them blessing when they come to the place where they can handle it.

Job's Daughters

Now, there is another surprise here, in verses 14 and 15, where the account now focuses upon the daughters of Job:

> And he called the name of the first Jemimah; and the name of the second Keziah; and the name of the third Keren-hap-puch. And in all the land there were no women so fair as Job's daughters; and their father gave them inheritance among their brothers.

If you are looking for girls' names, here are some excellent suggestions: Jemimah (that is sometimes connected with molasses); Keziah (that sounds like Kizzie in Alex Haley's book, *Roots*), and Keren-hap-puch. We will look at these significant names in a moment. The fascinating thing about this account is the focus on the daughters of Job, instead of the sons. In chapter one it was the sons who were in the forefront. They had a birthday party every year and invited their sisters to come and share with them. But here at the end of the book it is the daughters of Job. Now, being the father of four beautiful daughters myself, I know how Job must have felt about them. (It would have been a mistake to ask Job about his children, because you would have had to wait as he took out all their pictures to go through them with you!) He was proud of these daughters. In fact, he gave them an inheritance among their brothers, which was absolutely unheard of in the culture of that day.

If Women's Lib were looking for a text from Scripture, this would be an excellent one, for the whole point of the passage is that these daughters were made to share alike in the inheritance from their father. I believe that is symbolic, for this book is the story of a man who wanted to serve God, was upright and morally strong, and did his very best to do what God wanted, but was unconscious of the level of evil that was in his heart and life. On those terms he was living what we would call today the "natural life." The best of men at times will live moral, clean, upright lives. Job was like that. He was a true believer; I am not implying that he was not. But he had not yet discovered truth about God that would take him to that deeper level of life called the "spiritual life."

By the end of the book he has learned not to trust himself for anything at all. At the end he has learned that he cannot, in his own strength, do anything acceptable before God. He comes at last to the place where he has cast everything upon the grace of God and is taking his righteous standing before God to-

tally as God's gift to him. He is taking his stand on
the great Mediator of whom he himself has spoken
throughout this book. On those terms, as the New
Testament tells us, "if any man be in Christ there
is neither male nor female," but all share alike in
the glory of God and in the inheritance that is ours
in Jesus Christ our Lord. Spiritually, there are no
class or sex distinctions. That is what Job's granting
of an inheritance to his daughters, as well as to his
sons, is intended to signify.

I have suggested that the names of the daughters
are significant. Here are the meanings of them: *Jemimah* means "dove." As you know, throughout the
Scriptures, and even in our culture today, the dove
is the symbol of peace. *Keziah* is another spelling
of the word *cassia*. When the wise men brought their
gifts to the infant Jesus they brought gifts of cassia,
aloes, and myrrh, all of which were expensive, rare,
and beautiful fragrances. Cassia, therefore, is an in-
cense, or a fragrance. *Keren-happuch* literally means
"the horn of adornment," and is a reference to the
outward beauty that comes from an inward character.

What we have symbolized here is peace, fragrance, and beauty as the fruits of Job's trials. Surely,
as the text says, there were "none so fair in all the
land as these." The New Testament in Romans 5
tells us that suffering has this effect on those who
learn to take it as the evidence of God's love. Suffering, Paul says, produces patience, and patience produces character—beauty, fragrance, peace. And
character produces hope, hope that you are becom-
ing the kind of person you want to be. Hope does
not make us ashamed, Paul says. It leaves us confi-

dent and sure of our God and of the power and resources of the spiritual life.

The book ends on a note of contentment and peace:

> And after this Job lived a hundred and forty years, and saw his sons, and his sons' sons, four generations. And Job died, an old man, and full of days.

He was probably about seventy when the book opened, so he is now a really old man. What a picture of peace, a contented man. God has greatly blessed him. So God invites us also to forget about the distrust and fears, the anxieties of the past, the resentments we have been holding against others, the grudges, the criticisms—to put them all away and begin again. The question that is before us as we close this book (and I feel it deeply in my own heart), is, "On what basis am I going to live my life? Will it be on the old basis of it-all-depends-on-me, do-it-yourself goodness before God; trying my best to be pleasing to God and meaning it with all my heart, but never realizing the depths of evil with which I have to deal?" Or will it be to accept the gift of God which is waiting for me every day, fresh from his hand—the gift of forgiveness, of righteousness already mine, of a relationship in which he is my dear father and I am his cherished, beloved son? That I have, therefore, provided to me all day long— power to say "no" to evil and "yes" to truth and right. Will it be on that basis? If it is, my life will be characterized by peace, fragrance, and beauty. And so will yours. Or, if we insist on living it on the same old basis as before, we will find ourselves like these friends of Job, arousing the anger and the wrath of God. Though he is patient and merciful, our only escape will be to repent of our evil and rest upon the righteousness of our perfect Substitute, and return to God for the blessing he is waiting to give. That is the choice before us, every one of us.

Our hearts reflect these words, Lord Jesus. We sense the beauty of your life, the glory of your character. We know that it is your purpose to reproduce that in us, that we shall be like you. We thank you for what you are doing to bring it about. We thank you for the pressure, the pain, the trials, the disappointments, the afflictions that come upon us, Lord, by which you produce your likeness in us. Forgive us for our rebellion, for our complaints, for our murmuring against you. Help us to accept your tender mercies, Lord, and to see your loving, compassionate heart, and to bring praise, to the glory of our great God. We pray in your name, Amen.

13

Lessons from Job

The Book of Job is far too complex and profound to do a "once over lightly" treatment. In order not to miss its deepest lessons, let us review the account again. Since Job is probably the first Book of the Bible ever written it takes us back to the earliest days of man's redemptive history. As we have seen, Job was probably a contemporary of Abraham. He did not live in the Promised Land; he lived in another country of which we know very little, the ancient land of Uz. Yet his faith reflects that heritage of revelation which had verbally passed down to men and was widely scattered throughout the earth. It had come down through the stories men told each other, beginning with Adam and Eve, and through their children to the days of the Flood—then carried on beyond that by the sons of Noah. It is clear we have an early faith represented in the Book of Job. Yet, as we have seen in going through it, it is exactly in line with the greater revelation of Scripture which we come to in the Old and New Testaments.

This amazing book does what every book of the Bible does to some degree: it strips away illusions and permits us to see life as it really is. In my judgment, there is nothing more valuable about Scripture than that. We do not live very long without learning, often to our chagrin, that life is not what it really seems to be. We are surrounded by widely accepted philosophies and ideas that appear to be true but are not. We struggle with believing the Bible because it corrects these false conclusions and challenges the phony thinking of the world around us. That is why it is so important to let the Spirit of God set us straight by the Word of God, correcting our thinking and renewing our minds (Rom. 12:2).

The first surprise to hit us in Job is in chapter 1 where we are suddenly taken behind the scenes of this world and shown what goes on when a believer is being tried or tempted. We are all tried and tempted; we are all presented with alluring invitations to get involved with deadly and destructive things. We are pressured to lose our tempers, or lose our faith, and act in a way different than the Word of God says we should. We see those temptations as coming from adverse circumstances, perverse people, or both. We feel our trouble is that things are not working out the way we planned. If God would only straighten out these things and make them work according to our expectations, everything would be fine. Or if he would just get rid of some of these troublesome people around us!

The Weak Point in the Line

But in the Book of Job we see that this is not the whole story. What is really happening is that we have suddenly become the point in God's line of scrimmage (if I may use a football analogy) through which the devil and his angels have decided to try to run the ball. All the pressure of that well-trained, powerful team of evil is directed at us, and we suddenly discover we are the focus of his attack. That is what went on with Job, and what goes on in our lives as well. We are no longer sitting safely on the bench, watching the game and enjoying it. Suddenly, we find ourselves thrust right out in the middle of it. Our problem is that we forget this is what is happening. We see the situation only in terms of what is visible to us. In reading the Book of Job we must never forget what we are shown in the first chapter. And in facing the problems of our own lives, we must never forget that this book reveals what is happening to us in the midst of the troubles and temptations and pressures to which are being subjected.

Life is not a Sunday school picnic. The world around thinks it is, or ought to be—that somehow we deserve to have a good time and enjoy ourselves. But nothing is further from the Christian position. We are not here to have a good time. God gives us good times, but every one of them comes as a gift of his love and grace; they are never something we deserve. We are here to fight a battle against the powers of darkness. We are here to be engaged in an unending combat with powerful forces seeking to control human history. We have been called into battle. We must never forget that. That is why the Christian cannot plan his life, plan his retirement, as a worldling can. We are living different lives.

The older I grow the more I learn to see this present, earthly life of mine as I once thought of my time of service in the US Navy during World War II. I looked forward to the end of that time. I enjoyed it; it was an exciting time, but I looked forward to the end of it. Though I wanted to do well during that time, it was only a temporary period, and, for me, real life would begin when I got out. Or we can think of our present life very much as a boy might who goes away to college. He is there to learn something, to get ready for something, not primarily to enjoy himself. It is possible to have a lot of fun in college, and that is not wrong. But no one goes to school for that purpose—or at least they should not. College is not for spending money and having fun; college is for learning something. And so is life! That is why God has taught us what is going on behind the scenes right at the very beginning of the Book of Job. It is reality.

The Fruit of Something Deeper

The primary lesson of Job is what the book reveals about the nature of human evil. What is humanity like, in its basic character? As we have gone through this book we have seen how these friends speak to Job about various wicked people and almost always they speak in terms of murderers, thieves, rapists, fornicators, cruel tyrants—unjust, wretched people. These are the wicked, as these friends see them. But as we pursue the argument of the book, it becomes clear that the things they point out as wicked are really only the fruit of something deeper in human nature. They are coming from a deep-seated root of pride that expresses itself as independence, self-sufficiency, an "I've got what it takes, I can run my own life, I don't need help from anybody," kind of attitude. Jesus put it this way: "Out of the heart of man proceed murders and adulteries and fornication and hostility and anger." All the patently evil things come from the root of pride, which is evil in its purest form.

What we learn in this book is that pride is expressed, not only in terms of murder, thievery and robbery, but also (as we have seen in the three friends and even in Job himself), as bigotry and pompousness, as self-righteous legalism, as critical, judgmental attitudes and condemnation of others; as harsh, sarcastic words and vengeful, vindictive actions against someone else. There is wickedness, just as fully. So we learn that human evil is not confined to the criminals of the land. It is present in every heart, without exception, and it takes various forms. We are only deceiving ourselves when we say that the forms others take are wrong but ours is right. Pride is the root of all sin, and it can express itself in many various ways.

Coupled with this truth is what the book teaches us about the nature of faith. Job thought he was exercising faith when he obeyed God and did what was right, when it was clearly in his best interests to do so. Many people today think they are exercising great faith when they simply believe God is there—when they live their lives day by day with the recognition that God is watching and is present in their affairs. They do right because they know that if they do not, they will get into trouble. They call this living the Christian life—exercising faith. It is a form of faith, I grant that. It is believing, at least, in the invisible presence of God. But it is a weak faith. Those who live at such a level are serving God only when it is in their best interests to do so.

This was the accusation Satan hurled at God when Job was discussed. "Job serves you only because you take care of him. If you remove your hand of blessing from him, he'll curse you to your face." Many today serve God as long as he blesses them. The moment the blessing ceases, or difficulty or trial comes, they want to quit. Often I hear that someone has gotten into some difficulty or trouble has come, and he has turned his back on what he had professed about his Christian faith, throwing it all over, to live for himself and for the world. It is weak faith that only serves God when he blesses. We learn from this book that great faith, the kind which makes the world sit up and take notice, is revealed as we serve God when it is difficult to do so—when serving him is the hardest thing we can do. That is what we are taught in the Book of Job.

Remember the picture in the New Testament of the Sufferer of Gethsemane, who faced that hour in the garden, recognizing he was afraid of what was coming. He confessed to his disciples that his heart was exceedingly sorrowful within him, even unto death, and he asked three of them to pray for him and uphold him through a time of deep and terrible pressure. Yet, in that hour of anguish, though he prayed, "Father, if it be thy will, let this cup pass from me," reflecting his true humanity, nevertheless, by faith, he added the words, "not my will but thine be done." That is great faith. That we finally see exhibited here in Job. Though he trembles, though he falters, though he fails, the last thing he does is cling in helplessness to God. Thus Job ultimately becomes an example of faith. Great faith is exercised when we feel we are being the least faithful, when we are so weak that we cannot do anything but cling. In that moment, all heaven is looking and rejoicing at the greatness of our faith.

Fallen Man at His Best

All this adds up to the true view, then, of the nature of fallen man. Man in the flesh appears at his best in the person of Job. When this book opens, we have a beautiful picture of a highly respected and greatly honored man; a sincere, moral, devoted, selfless, godly man who spends his time doing good deeds and helping many people, obviously intent upon doing what God wants. We would call him a deserving man, infinitely deserving of God's blessing, because he so faithfully served and followed him. There are many like that today who are not even Christians and yet who live on those terms. They are often, in a sense, godly people in that they recognize there is a God and try to follow him. They are apparently devoted and selfless people, and represent fallen man at his very best.

But what this book is designed to do is strip away the outward appearances and show us Job as he really is. He finally came to see himself as self-deceived. He imagined he had resources in himself to handle life and its problems which he really did not have. This is one of the tremendous lessons of the book. We, too, imagine we have power to stand and be true to what we believe. We are like boastful, blustering Peter, who said to the Lord Jesus, "I will never deny you. I will lay down my life for you." He meant every word of it; yet, when the hour of temptation struck, he found himself as weak as putty. He too came to realize, as Job did, that he had no resources to stand in himself, that God had to hold him, or he would never be held. Out of his weakness came his strength.

This book shows us how Job discovered he was a lover of status and prestige. When God took away his position in the community he began to think longingly of those days when he had a position of high honor and dignity, when he could walk out into the community and people bowed before him

and respected him. Job discovered that he liked that.
It was what made him keep on serving God. When
all that disappeared, he found himself querulous and
angry, upset because he had been denied what he
thought was his right. The book teaches us that our
hearts, more than we can understand, seek to share
glory with God. We really do not want to serve God
unless we get glory for ourselves out of it. That is
often the reason why we do things—because we are
motivated by a desire for status and prestige in the
eyes of others. All this is stripped away from Job.
As we read this book we discover that God seems
to come across as somewhat smaller than Job himself,
that Job's self-vindication and self-justification makes
God look less than he is. This is the terrible evil of
that attitude. It robs God of his glory. Paul, in 1
Corinthians, reminds us, "No flesh shall glory in
God's presence." But we find this attitude in our
own lives frequently. How this book reveals it to us!

The great theme of the book—and the one for
which it is world-famous—is its treatment of the reason for suffering in the Christian life. None of us
protests when we are told that suffering is sent by
God to punish wrongdoers. We have a long list of
names we would like to present to God of people
who deserve punishment. It is eminently just for
God to punish such wrongdoers with suffering, we
think. People who hurt others and are vicious, cruel
and wicked ought to be made to suffer for what they
do. Our whole system of justice is built upon that
principle. That is why we put men and women in
jail or fine them, because we are trying to carry out
justice by punishing wrongdoing. That satisfies our
sense of justice—except when we happen to be the
wrongdoers receiving the punishment! Then, of
course, it is all very unfair.

We can even handle it when the Bible teaches that suffering is sent to awaken us when we tend to go astray. Even though we are saints, suffering is sometimes sent to get our attention. We can understand that, too. We have all had the experience of drifting away from God and thinking everything is going fine. We are drifting along and doing OK (we think), when suddenly some catastrophe strikes, some terrible trouble comes. At first we resent it, complain bitterly, and ask "why should this happen?" But it keeps on, and finally we begin to hear what God is saying. When we are quiet we see things that are wrong. Much of this is happening in Job, and we understand that.

But that is not all the Book of Job teaches us about suffering. There is something far greater than that. This book reveals something that should have been obvious to us from our reading of the Gospels—the fact that Jesus suffered. Obviously, Jesus did not suffer because he was a wrongdoer, nor did he suffer because he needed to have his attention captured by God. He was always sensitively responsive to the Father's will, and always did what was pleasing in his sight. Yet his life was filled with suffering from beginning to end—rejection, misunderstanding, disappointment, cruelty, harsh words and unjust treatment—all the way through. He thoroughly merited the description of the Old Testament—"a man of sorrows, and acquainted with grief."

Satan Revealed As a Liar

Why did he suffer? He suffered because suffering is also a way of allowing God to demonstrate that Satan is a liar and a cheat. Satan had made proclamation before all the universe that men serve God only

because God blesses them. He said, "If you remove
the blessing, men will curse God to his face." Man
does not see any intrinsic value in God himself, but
it is only his own self-interest that makes him serve
God. Far too often believers have confirmed that
lie of Satan. But in the case of Job, and, frequently
in our own experience, suffering is sent to prove
that Satan is wrong, that God will be served even
when he does not bless any longer, because he is
God, and he is worthy of the praise and the honor
and service of men. That is why Jesus suffered. He
suffered as a demonstration to all mankind that God
was still God and was worthy of service no matter
what happened.

This is why death meant nothing to the Lord. He
despised the cross, we are told, "Having his eye fas-
tened on the joy which was beyond, he despised
the cross," and went on to become the great Sufferer
of Calvary. Job teaches us that suffering is a means
by which evil is answered, and God vindicated. It
is a high and holy and glorious privilege granted
to some Christians to uphold the glory of God in
the midst of the accusations of the devil in this world.
May we learn to see suffering in that way. Sometimes
we eminently deserve it. Sometimes it comes because of our misdeeds, to awaken us. But sometimes
it is granted to us because it is a high and holy privilege we have, to do what Paul calls sharing the sufferings of Christ, "filling up that which is lacking in
the sufferings of Christ, for his body's sake, which
is the church."

Some years ago I was introduced to a woman who
had just lost her husband and her son in an auto
accident. Her heart was broken; she was devastated
by this double loss that had suddenly come into her
life. When I went to see her she was weeping, hardly

even able to speak because she was so overcome by her grief. Someone had asked me to try to comfort her but I wondered what to say to her. Looking to God in prayer, I laid my hand on her shoulder and said, "You have been given a very high and holy honor." Glancing up through her tears, she said to me, "What do you mean?" I sat down with her and went through some of the Scriptures, pointing out to her that we are given the privilege of suffering for Christ. Paul puts it that way to the Philippians: "It has been given on behalf of Christ, not only to believe on him, but also to suffer for his name's sake." I pointed out to her that God had given her the privilege of bearing difficulty and trial, given her an opportunity to demonstrate that his strength and his love and his grace will continue, despite all the outward circumstances, even in the worst of things which life can throw at us. As we talked together, a new look came on her face. She said to me, "I see what you mean." We prayed together and I left her. Later, I heard that her life was such a radiant testimony throughout this time of struggle that hundreds of people were touched and saw their own sufferings in a different light as a result.

I once went to see a Christian couple who had just had a mongoloid baby. I said something very similar to them: "God has called you into very high privilege in giving you this. You're being given a chance to demonstrate something very few other Christians are asked to bear. If you will see it in that light, what a difference it will make." The couple did take it that way, and their dealings with their child as he has grown have been a constant testimony to scores of people of the goodness and greatness of God.

Job is teaching us, by means of the symbolism of

these two great beasts, Behemoth and Leviathan, how God handles evil. What God is saying to Job is, "Look, you've had a part in this with me. Your suffering, your unexplained torment, the physical affliction you've been going through, have been the means by which I have been able to lay hold of these two ferocious powers to control them, regulate them, and keep them in bounds in the world. You have been the instrument of it." Job, therefore, was given the tremendous glory of bearing suffering for the Lord's sake.

Then, of course, the greatest theme of all in this Book of Job, and the one I hope we will remember more than anything else, is that the book reveals to us the character of God himself. God often appears to us as a cold, impersonal Being, distant from us, uncaring; he is pictured as even ruthless and vindictive, demanding many things from us—powerful, but without compassion. I am sure if you conducted a poll you would find that this is the commonest view of God in the world today. That is the common concept of what is often called the "Old Testament God"—as though God were two kinds of Beings, one for the Old Testament and one for the New. But what this book shows us is that behind that appearance (even Job saw him that way for a while), God is always exactly the same, not ruthless and cold, but compassionately aware of our problems. He is deeply concerned about us, carefully controlling everything that touches us, limiting the power of Satan according to his knowledge of how much we can bear. He is patient, forgiving, and ultimately responsible for everything that happens.

In the beginning of this book we find three characters: God, Satan and Job. By the end of the book,

Satan has faded into the background, completely disappeared. All we have left is God, standing before Job with his arms akimbo, saying to him, "All right, Job, I'm responsible. Any questions?" When Job begins to see what God is working out in his vast, cosmic purposes, and what he is making possible by means of Job's sufferings, he has no questions to ask whatsoever. The final view of God in this book is of a Being of incredible wisdom who puts things together far beyond the dreams and imaginations of man; who is working out magnificent purposes of infinite delight and joy that he will give to us if we wait for his ends to be fully accomplished.

This book mentions a time when "the sons of God shouted with joy" at the creation of the world. But other scriptures tell us about a time that is coming when "the sons of God will be revealed." Paul calls it "the manifestation of the sons of God," when all creation will shout in a greater glory than was ever hailed at creation. It will be the new creation, the new thing God has brought into being by means of the sufferings, the trials, and the tribulations of this present scene. That is why Scripture speaks in numerous passages about "this slight momentary affliction preparing for us an eternal weight of glory beyond all comparison," and of how "the sufferings of this present time are not worthy to be compared with the glory that will be revealed in us." When that great day breaks, the one thing for which we will be infinitely thankful, the one thing above all others which will thrill us and cheer us and cause us to glory, is this: out of all the created universe we were chosen to be the ones who bore the name of God in the hour of danger and affliction, problem and trial. There is no higher honor than that. This is what Jesus means when he says, "Blessed are you, when men persecute you and say all manner of evil against you falsely, for my name's sake. Rejoice, and be exceeding glad, for great is your honor before the Father. For so persecuted they the prophets who were before you."

Now, the sufferings of Christ involve more than bearing reproach for his name's sake. It also involves illness, affliction, accident, the so-called handicaps with which people are born—all this becomes part of sharing the sufferings of Christ if we take them as a privilege and not as a reproach. We must view life as God sees it, seeing this as only a temporary time when we have a great opportunity to bear honor for Christ that we will never have again. Never again in all eternity will we ever have the privilege of bearing suffering for his name's sake in a day of reproach. So, as we are called to this suffering, I pray that this Book of Job will help us to understand the realities of life, the greatness of the privilege accorded to us, and the richness of glory God heaps upon us when he allows us to suffer for his name's sake.

Our Father, words fail us to express what we feel in our hearts. We do count it indeed a mighty privilege to bear reproach for your name's sake. We know that the day is coming when that will be our chief joy, that will be the treasure that we have laid up in heaven. We hope, Lord, that it will be a rich treasure indeed, that we will stop our complaining and griping about what you send, and count it a great joy to bear suffering and reproach for your name's sake, sharing the sufferings of Christ, that we may also share in the glory which is to follow. We ask in his name, Amen.